WITHDRAWN

HOW TO REDUCE YOUR REAL ESTATE TAXES

HOW TO REDUCE YOUR REAL ESTATE TAXES

SAMUEL T. BARASH

**ARCO PUBLISHING, INC.
NEW YORK**

Published by Arco Publishing, Inc.
219 Park Avenue South, New York, N.Y. 10003

Copyright © 1979 by Samuel T. Barash

Library of Congress Cataloging in Publication Data
  Barash, Samuel T   1921-
    How to reduce your real estate taxes.

    Includes index.
    1. Property tax—United States—Handbooks, manuals, etc.
I. Title HJ4120.B37   336.2'2'0973   78-11224

ISBN O-668-04715-1 (Library Edition)
ISBN O-668-04720-8 (Paper Edition)

Printed in the United States of America

ACKNOWLEDGMENT

With particular thanks to Mike Fogarty, Ted Nardin, Alvin Lucas, Merebeth Smith, Mal Davidson, Esq. and with love and gratitude to Julia Barash, Esq. and Kit Barash, helpmate, for their patience and help.

Contents

Contents

How This Book Can Reduce Your Property Taxes

Yes, you can get your property taxes reduced.

Most of us, however, don't take the time to look over our property assessments and appeal them if wrong. Most appeals result in reductions. Yet the total number of appeals is small compared to those who pay property taxes which are illegal, in error, unequal, unfair and too high.

In one town of 14,000, with a competent, dedicated, over-worked assessor, only 18 homeowners recently appealed for reduced assessments on Grievance Day. Six of these 18 assessments were found wrong and were reduced up to $4,300 each in assessment. Tax savings— each year—ranged up to $175 per home.

When you own your home or other real estate property, you become the most "dumped-on" of all consumer-taxpayers. Property taxes reach new highs each year. You can't shop around in different supermarkets for lower taxes. You can't move your property to escape unfair, too high taxes.

Tax rebellion is spreading. In New York State, everyone in one small town has become a minister by mail ordination to escape property taxes. In California, the voters recently passed the "Jarvis Initiative" by referendum vote which limited property taxes to 1% of property value there even though they were thereby curtailing their own public services. These instances are extreme examples of the frustration property owners are experiencing as they see their taxes double, triple and more.

As an individual property owner taxpayer, you don't have to just sit and wait for a "Boston Tea Party" to happen in your area. Even Californians still are not guaranteed that their individual property taxes will be fair within their ceiling of 1% of their inflated market values.

What you can do is stand up for a fair assessment on your property. Should you win your appeal, and most people do, you can save a lot of money—hundreds of dollars a year or even more—if you follow the plan I've mapped out in this book. Other homeowners and owners of other kinds of real property have done it. You can do it too.

Item—Herbert _____ of _____, home assessed for $72,000. Appealed, claiming overassessment based on extraordinarily high heating costs because his modern glass-front ranch-style house was built during a prior era of lower energy costs, reducing market appeal and value. Assessment reduced to $55,000. Net savings *each* year in taxes—$510.

Item—Sam _____ of _____, home assessed for $62,-000. Appealed, claiming overassessment based on lower sales of similar properties. Assessment reduced to $59,000. Net savings *each* year in taxes—$160.

Item—Mark _____ of _____, owner of 64.4 acres of land, assessed for $122,500. Appealed, claiming gross over-assessment of mainly steep, non-developable land and lower sales of comparable land parcels. Assessment reduced to $89,500. Net current tax savings *each* year— $1,163.

Item—Marvin _____ of _____, owner of a large bungalow colony assessed for one million dollars, appealed, claiming reduced net income and lower sales of comparable properties. Assessment reduced to $776,000. Received $15,600 tax *refund*.

I know these people and their properties. They are but a few examples of the real estate tax cash which can be saved with and without experts. You can do it too.

Real estate appraisers and attorneys are experts. They charge high fees for assessment appeals. However, the owner is the greatest expert of all. After all, you know your property and neighborhood best. This book shows how to use your own expertise to save appeal fees and reduce your property taxes. You paint and repair your own house. You can also appeal-it-yourself to lower your property assessment and save property tax dollars.

There are some facts you have to know first. For example, did you know that—

1. The property taxes you pay are based on an assessment of your property. Yet assessments have often been made illegally and incorrectly on the wrong property.

2. This assessment is supposed to be based on what your property is worth in the open real estate market. Actually, most assessments are far removed from actual market value.

3. If your tax bill says $20,000 assessment and you know your house is worth $45,000, does that mean your taxes are not too high? Wrong! Practically all assessments are for much less than market value. Your assessment could seem low and yet cause you to pay hundreds of dollars in too high property taxes—each year.

4. Your assessment and real estate taxes are supposed to be similar to your neighbors' who have similar properties. In too many assessments, similar properties are assessed as if they were on different planets.

5. Assessors legally set down how much your property is worth and therefore how much property taxes you pay. Yet most assessors don't have to know anything at all about assessing to be assessors. In fact, most assessors don't have to know anything. Some don't even have to know how to read.

This book shows how you can reduce your property taxes. It breaks down assessors' and appraisers' jargon into plain English. It gives clear step-by-step procedures on what you have to do to get your assessment reduced and your taxes lowered. It is organized as an *action plan* you can follow step-by-step.

There are introductory chapters on how the assessment system works, how you are assessed. Then there is a chapter listing 40 ways the assessor may have made a mistake on your assessment—and the 40 grounds for appeal.

The rest of the book tells exactly—

1. How you research an appeal.

2. How you check for errors in assessors' records on your property.

3. How you compare your property to your neighbors' and to similar properties to make sure you are being assessed with an even hand.

4. How you put it all together. How you stand up and present your case to the Grievance Committee.

5. How you go to the next appeal stage if you get turned down.

6. If all else fails, when to hire a lawyer to go to court if the potential savings are worth it. (One of my clients even represented himself in court and won his suit on settlement. Total legal cost—$5.00 filing fee for Notice of Protest.)

Throughout the book there are also completed model complaint forms, construction inspection checklists and appraisal guides to help you research and prepare your appeal. The guides and checklists should also help you locate basic construction faults like termites or settlement or location influences which should assist your claim for reduction in assessment. The completed complaint forms will help you prepare your own appeal.

Finally, there is an Appendix with a collection of useful information on assessments and appeals. There are typical assessment appeal procedures on a state-by-state basis. There is a 50-state address list of state assessment offices if you want specific additional information on your own state's regulations. An assessment/tax dictionary is also appended to help you through some of the assessment system's special terminology. And there is an index to help you find the data you need in this book.

You will find what you need to know here to reduce your property taxes. All you have to do is take that first step—appeal!

CHAPTER 1

How You Are Assessed on Your Property

This first chapter gives you the theory of the real property assessment/tax system. It shows how the system is supposed to work and how it really works. So that you can better understand how to reduce your ever-increasing real estate taxes, there is also a section which defines basic assessment tax words. There are details on what the assessor does and how he assesses your property. Finally, you will see here the system's end result—how these assessments are used to take your money when property taxes are collected.

THE THEORY OF THE PROPERTY TAX SYSTEM

Land, houses and slaves were first taxed 2400 years ago in ancient Greece. In 1646, the colony of Massachusetts began collecting property taxes. During all these centuries of real estate taxes, the system hasn't really gotten accepted or better. No one likes to pay taxes, especially when they get more unequal and unfair each year.

In theory, the property tax is fair since it taxes those of us whose property causes a need for community services like roads, utilities, schools, fire and police protection. Theoretically, it is also fair because property owners pay taxes proportionate to the value of the property they own. Thus, according to the theory, the taxes which are fairly collected from you are then used to support the government and school services you need. The system has progressed a bit from its origin. Real estate property is now mainly taxed, not personal property—such as slaves. Some critics say this is so because it's hard to get a true account of personal property while real estate is fixed in place and can't be hidden from tax collector. Other critics have even said that slaves are still taxed, only now they are not personal property—just property owners, chained to and unable to escape unfair taxes on their immovable real estate.

How It's Supposed to Work

Property taxes are *ad valorem*, an old Latin word which means, "according to value." In other words, an ad valorem tax is a tax which is levied (placed) against property in proportion to the value of the property which is the subject of the assessment. It is supposed to be a property tax and not a people tax.

Most states (see Appendix) have ad valorem tax assessments based upon the full value concept. This means that assessments are supposed to be placed on all properties at the full value of each property. Actually, even in those states, full value assessments are rare. Often, there is resistance from local assessors who fear removal from office if they "up" taxpayers assessments. Antique assessing methods make it impossible for assessors to keep up with individual property value changes or annual inflation in property values. The result is that most assessments are made at less than market value each year.

So what difference does it make? defenders of the system ask. If the assessment is at any fraction of the actual market value of the property, then just raise the *tax rate*, they say. Witness the following arithmetic:

$100,000 (full value) × $20 per $1000 tax rate =
$2000 (tax bill)
or
$25,000 (@25% assessment) × $80 per $1000 rate =
$2000 (tax bill)

This is the theory of the taxing system, and we deal here only with real property, not personal property. Unfortunately for all of us who own homes or other real estate, this theory looks good only in numbers on paper. In reality, as shown below, it works mainly to confuse and make you think you are not over-paying your taxes.

How the System Actually Works

Admittedly, any assessor faces a formidable task each year with poor tools. Originally a state tax, the property tax has become a local tax levied by some 65,000 taxing districts, including political municipalities, schools, special districts like sewer, water, etc. Since states now get their revenue mainly from income and sales taxes, many states give very little guidance to the local assessor. Even when there is a state manual of standards, each assessor—who is usually elected, sometimes appointed—in most areas needs no experience or education to be an assessor (see Appendix I). So when he comes into office, the assessor finds some thousands or tens of thousands of properties in his district, each needing assessment each year. The record cards rarely are complete; the data on each property is never fully current. In most localities, there aren't even tax maps to identify each property. Some states offer localities the benefits of modern computerized data recording and assessing systems, but most local assessors, particularly in suburban and rural areas, do not use these services. Even if computers are used, they are often a mixed blessing insofar as property owner appeals are concerned. The taxpayer can always make an appointment to discuss his assessment records and values with the assessor. How do you argue with a computer?

With all these problems, is it any wonder that fractional assessment (assessing at a percentage of market value) is the name of the game? If it hadn't evolved, some other method would have had to have been invented to mystify the taxpayer.

Also, this type of mass appraising which is called assessing has built-in time and political problems. Most assessors solve the problems by applying a cost index factor across the board on all properties in their district or by only increasing assessments on properties that are sold.

Appendix No. 1 gives data on the taxing procedures in the 50 states. All these procedures actually can be summarized in practically all localities as follows:

Step 1—Each year, your property is listed along with all other properties in the taxing district.

Step 2—It is then assessed (valued) and issued on a tax roll with all others on a legal date once a year.

Step 3—The tax rate is then set by dividing the total value on the tax roll by the total budget (expected expenses) of the political or other district. Definite calendar dates are set for this tax levy because the tax moneys have to come in on time to pay budget expenses in an orderly manner.

Step 4—You pay.

These are uniform basic procedures everywhere. And if you don't pay, as in Step 4, they "sell" the tax lien (what you owe) and your property is eventually taken away from you.

So it is important to know not only the theory but also the actual assessment practice. Not only fractional assessments, but incomplete data, incompetent, overworked assessors, favoritism, varying rates for varying types of property—all compound the problem and cause unequal, unfair assessments and taxes. Commercial-industrial properties are often under-assessed deliberately in one community compared to residential properties and vice-versa in another community. Many times the assessor's desire to get re-elected is much more influential than market value and equity.

The end result is that the system actually works to make assessments and taxes unequal and unfair. Chapter 2 details all those reasons why your assessment can be so wrong.

Definitions of Assessment, Assessment Rate, "Ad Valorem" Tax, etc.

Appendix III has a full assessment/tax dictionary and glossary. However, there are certain special words which are basic to your understanding and coping with this archaic and deliberately mystifying process:

ASSESSMENT—The value of a property which is multiplied by a tax rate to get the dollar tax amount.

ASSESSMENT RATE—Either by law or by practice, that percentage of market value at which properties in a district are assessed.

AD VALOREM TAX—A tax which is based on the value of the property.

FULL VALUE—Describes those regulations which require that assessments be at full market value.

HIGHEST AND BEST USE—Property generally has to be assessed for its best, most profitable use.

MARKET VALUE—Market value is that amount which a property will bring in the open market from a ready willing and able buyer and a willing seller, neither acting under duress nor constraint.

MILL—Is 1000th of a dollar. A tax rate of 10 mills is 1 cent per dollar of assessed value. It can be stated in dollars per 100 or 1000.

TAX RATE—This rate is secured by dividing the total assessed value of the district into the tax levy and is usually expressed in dollars per hundred or per thousand. This rate is then multiplied by the assessed value to get amount of taxes on each property. For example, $1,500,000 tax levy ÷ $75,000,000 = $20 per $1000 tax rate. Thus, a house assessed @ $50,000 multiplied by $20 tax rate would pay $1000 a year taxes.

REPLACEMENT COST—The amount it would cost to replace the building with similar materials today, less depreciation for age, function, declining neighborhood values, etc. This approach to value is still used by most assessors.

INCOME APPROACH—A standard appraisal approach to value, generally used for commercial, industrial and large multiple dwellings when similar property sales are not available. The net income, real or expected, is multiplied by a capitalization factor to get total property value. This approach is not useful for 1-4 family dwellings.

WHAT THE ASSESSOR DOES

The assessor uses all these special words and concepts to assess your property. He does his job based on state laws which generally make him the boss of assessments once he is elected or appointed. Usually, in most states, he is the final authority on establishing original assessments before appeal. In a few localities, he even sits on appeal boards.

So what he does and how he does his job is critically important to your property taxes. This is what an assessor does in practically all districts:

1. He *receives information* and copies of deeds on all real property sales in his district.

2. He *maintains* and updates public assessment record files on each property, based usually on a percentage of current market value.

3. He *delivers* his assessment roll for publication by the legal date in his locality each year.

4. He is *responsible* for at least the initial receipt and processing of all appeals on his assessments.

HOW YOUR PROPERTY IS ASSESSED

We have shown how most assessors, once elected or appointed, get very little guidance and are generally responsible to no one in their locality or in their state.

This makes for a high degree of individuality in assessment practices and a low degree of uniformity.

Appendix No. 1 lists those states which furnish assessment manuals to their thousands of assessors. Even in the few states which do give such guidance, these manuals are generally out-dated, not kept up and are usually based on construction costs rather than market sales. The few states which offer computerized output of sales data generally find local assessors unwilling to switch to these modern methods. The majority of states do not even make these attempts to ensure uniformity. (See Appendix I)

Some states use so-called "equalization" techniques to make taxes more uniform, district to district. These equalization (assessment to sales) ratios are derived by statistically comparing selling prices of properties with assessed values of these sold properties. The resultant ratio is then applied by locality as an adjustment factor to "equalize" taxes which vary from district to district. Simply, if you own a home in Yourtown and your cousin owns his home in Histown, such states will compare the assessments in each town to actual sales, then hand out state aid moneys based on these ratios to equalize any differences. This is done annually for all communities in most states.

If your property is a *home*, assessors in some localities generally will try to assess it based on current market value using recent sales of similar properties. Of course, the asssessor then has to apply the required percentage of full value as appropriate in his area. If you own *income producing* property like stores, industrial or apartment buildings, he will use the Income Approach by capitalizing at a "fair return," the net income of the property. (See Definitions.) In many areas though, whether home, commercial or industrial, the assessors still use the old-fashioned Cost Replacement Approach, either in conjunction with the Market Approach or Income Approach or alone. This cost method has been a preferred assessment method for many years because it is easy to apply to a mass of individual properties. However, it is particularly difficult to defend as a uniform assessment tool because of the constant adjustments which have to be made for constantly changing construction costs and materials. There is also the high degree of assessor "guesstimating" on depreciation amounts which is basic to the Cost Approach.

As stated, commercial and industrial properties are usually assessed by calculating how much net income they produce rather than by what it would cost to replace or by comparison with what similar nearby properties have sold for recently. However, this often leads to even further inequity. During inflation, home assessments usually go up based on increased value while industrial/commercial assessments may go down based on the same inflation-increased expenses which reduce their net income and, consequently, value.

The land portion of your property is always valued separately from building improvements in assessing practice. In typical city or development plots, these lots are generally valued on a front (road) foot basis adjusted by depth of lot. (See the Land Depth Table which follows later and which is supposed to adjust for less valuable excess or deficient depth.) The theory underlying these adjustment tables is that the front part of the lot is the more valuable. These tables make for quick handling of the many land parcels which need assessing. Unfortunately, as with cost manuals which are used to assess buildings, it becomes easier for the assessor to use such tables and "cost" arithmetic to assess lots by so called "effective" depth, width and corner "influence" than to keep up with actual lot sales to maintain lot assessments on a current, fair and uniform basis.

For example, your home is on an interior 60′ × 140′ plot. Values in the area are @ $200 per front foot for a 120′ standard plot, according to the assessor. He then does the following calculations to arrive at lot value:

60′ × $200 × 1.08 (from table) = $12,960 Lot Value

(SELECTED FACTORS)
TYPICAL 120′ STANDARD LOT
DEPTH TABLE

Depth	Factor	Depth	Factor	Depth	Factor	Depth	Factor
80	.82	103	.92	126	1.02	149	1.11
81	.82	104	.93	127	1.02	150	1.11
82	.83	105	.94	128	1.03	151	1.11
83	.83	106	.94	129	1.03	152	1.12
84	.84	107	.95	130	1.04	153	1.12
85	.84	108	.95	131	1.04	154	1.12
86	.85	109	.96	132	1.05	155	1.13
87	.85	110	.96	133	1.05	156	1.13
88	.86	111	.97	134	1.05	157	1.13
89	.86	112	.97	135	1.06	158	1.13
90	.87	113	.98	136	1.06	159	1.14
91	.87	114	.99	137	1.07	160	1.14
92	.87	115	.99	138	1.07		
93	.88	116	.99	139	1.07		
94	.88	117	1.00	140	1.08		
95	.89	118	1.00	141	1.08		
96	.89	119	1.00	142	1.08		
97	.90	*120*	*1.00*	143	1.09		
98	.90	121	1.01	144	1.09		
99	.91	122	1.01	145	1.09		
100	.91	123	1.01	146	1.10		
101	.91	124	1.02	147	1.10		
102	.92	125	1.02	148	1.10		

Whenever assessments become too far out of line because of these antiquated methods or whenever a court decision or too many irate taxpayers require that something be done, most districts and assessors usually call for reassessment help. This usually involves revaluations of the whole district, rarely by the assessor himself, usually by private appraisal companies hired at so much per parcel. Often this revaluation is done because politically it is usually wiser to raise assessments rather than the tax rate which affects everyone and always excites voter reaction. Unfortunately, the history of many revaluations done by private assessment companies is that they often are neither fair nor equitable. And even these so-called current 100% revaluations rarely stay current for longer than the year they are done.

Who Uses Assessments to Collect Taxes?

You are the end of the line of this assessment/tax process. You have to come up with the tax money each year which is demanded by the tax collector under pain of foreclosure. This ancient way of guessing at property values was alright supposedly when there were fewer property owners and less expensive properties. During the past three decades our country has become suburbanized and now there are many more community, school and other local costs in our modern complex suburban-urban society. Now the tax collector takes the assessment roll from the assessor each year, punches the roll's total dollars into his calculator, divides by his communities budget, and out comes your tax rate—up to 5% and more effectively of the value of your property.

Yet, you can't refuse to pay the collector because he will only foreclose and take away the other 95% of your property. You have to unravel this archaic, deliberately mystifying process, find the man at the beginning of the process—not the collector, but the assessor. You, as an individual, may not be able to change this chaotic system. You certainly can make sure you are assessed uniformly with your neighbors and that you are paying no more than your fair share each year. The stakes are now too high to give up because the system is hopeless. We're talking of effective tax rates today approaching and exceeding 5% of the market value of your property and 15% of average income.

CHAPTER 2

Why Your Assessment Can Be So Wrong

Chapter 1 showed how your property is assessed. This companion chapter introduces all the built-in reasons which cause errors and inequities in your assessment and taxes. Information is given here on those who do the job—the tens of thousands of assessors who are mainly over-worked, under-paid and hardly ever qualified to do assessment work. You will also find here that there are more than 65,000 taxing districts, each one rarely assessing uniformly within its own area or compared to its neighbors. There is a section on how politics too often complicate assessment arithmetic. There is data here too on why commercial/industrial properties are often under-assessed compared to residential and vice versa. The modern phenomenon of tax exemptions causing tax rebellions by taxpayers is explored in this chapter. There is an analysis of why this archaic system

18

appears hopelessly incapable of coping with its assessment job. And most important nowadays to your pocketbook, there are warnings here on why 100% revaluations often double your taxes. Finally, you will see here how recent important court decisions are affecting your taxes.

Over-worked, Underpaid and Under-qualified Assessors

The assessor works mainly alone in this difficult field, beset by irate taxpayer-voters. He must constantly attempt to keep his many properties current for each tax roll. He suffers often from inaccuracies in prior public record descriptions of property improvements and is generally unable legally to enter individual premises to verify inaccuracies or recent improvements. He gets recorded deed copies when properties are sold and can estimate sales price by adding up the tax stamps on these deeds but he must verify each sale for it to have value meaning. Many times, with his mass of data, ancient forms of property record keeping and legal deadlines, this is just not possible.

Faced with such impossible workload, annual deadlines and archaic methods, it is no wonder that there is also a large turnover among many of these tens of thousands of local assessors. Many of them work part time; some sit on legal assessment boards of three, probably to spread the responsibility and complaint backlash. The vast majority are not only underpaid considering their legal responsibilities but also not qualified to be assessors. Very few of these mainly elected, some appointed assessors have to meet any experience or educational requirements, including even the ability to read and write. (See Appendix I.)

More Than 65,000 Taxing Localities

We are one nation. However, for property tax purposes, we are divisible into 50 states, some of which try, mainly unsuccessfully, to supervise local assessment and taxes. We are further divisible into more than 65,000 taxing units—political geographic subdivisions such as cities, villages, counties, towns, and school districts, road districts, sewer districts, lighting districts, health districts, fire districts, etc., etc. These many taxing authorities who take a cut of your tax pie seem endless and ever-growing. The following is a multi-authority example from the author's own tax bill which even includes such an exotic modern environmental tax entity as an Aquatic Growth District which pays for underwater mowing and collecting weed growth in the local lake.

This type of notice is usually sent with the tax bill to explain the bill. However, sometimes neither the notice nor the bill is received by the taxpayer—because it gets lost in the mails or perhaps sent to the bank which holds the mortgage or never sent at all because of poor bookkeeping. Even if never received, the tax is still due. Many localities are required by law to notify taxpayers whenever their assessments are raised. Some are not required to notify. Some do it only by publishing the tax roll or just posting it in a public place. Again, despite requirements or methods or non-receipt, the taxpayer has to meet his locality's legal deadline for contesting increases even if he doesn't know about the increase or the deadline. You pay the taxes; you have to do the legwork to find out what's going on. Appendix I of this book, with its state-by-state appeal filings table, will help. However, you have to regularly, each year or as often as is necessary, stay fully informed generally on assessment pro-

TOWN OF MONROE
COLLECTOR'S TAX NOTICE

Notice is hereby given that I, the undersigned Collector of Taxes of the Town of Monroe, Orange County, New York, have duly received the tax roll and warrant for the collection of taxes for the present fiscal year and that I will attend from 9 A. M. to 4 P. M., at Town Hall, 15 Lake Street, Monroe, N. Y., on Mondays through Fridays during the month of January, for 30 days from this date for the purpose of receiving the taxes assessed upon such roll.

Taxes may be paid on or before January 31, 1978 without charge or interest. On all such taxes remaining unpaid after such date one percent will be added for the first month and an additional one-half percent for each month and fraction thereafter until the return of unpaid taxes is made to the County Treasurer, pursuant to law, on April 1st, 1978,

65 OR OVER?

You may be eligible for Senior Citizens Tax Exemptions. Call Meribeth Smith, Assessor at 782-8221, or write 15 Lake Street, Monroe.

FORD S. RELYEA, 3rd, Collector

Dated: December 31, 1977.

RATES

GENERAL { State .... 9.11 }
{ County .... 2,03 } $11.14
{ Town .... }

Consolidated Bd. Health	.02
Part Town	.55
Town Highway	3.99
Fire Protection	.81
Town Light District	.22
LRH Rd. Imp. (Per Unit)	6.61
Acorn Hill Rd. Imp. (Per Unit)	107.33
Cooper St. Rd. Imp. (Per Unit)	134.83
Centerhill Rd. Imp. (Per Unit)	225.81
St. George Rd., Imp. (Per Unit)	42.23
Walton Ter. Rd. Imp. (Per Unit)	32.07
Idle Hour Park Rd. Imp. (Per Unit)	8.66
Aquatic Growth Dist. #6	1.08
Aquatic Growth Dist. #8	1.35
Water District #1	128.36
WD No. 2 & SD No. 7	12.15
Sewer Bonds	1.10407
Sewer Laterals	1.52859

THIS IS NOT A BILL

PLEASE RETURN BILL WITH REMITTANCE

cedures in your locality and on your assessment records in particular.

Besides these constantly multiplying tax districts which demand portions of your tax rates, this "Balkanization" of tens of thousands of assessing jurisdiction makes uniformity and equity in tax rates a practical impossibility among adjoining districts as well as within each district. This hodge-podge of political, school and other authorities all are given the legal right to tax your property but very few are guided or controlled to see that similar properties pay similar fair taxes. They are mainly all on their own when they assess your property. And so are you when you have to pay the resulting taxes.

How Politics Often Complicates Assessment Arithmetic

It sounds good that a local person, one of your neighbors, assesses your property for property tax purposes rather than a faraway agency like IRS which does the same for your income taxes. The political reality is not good at all.

For many years, even into these modern times, the assessor's job has been politically tainted. Appendix I clearly shows that most assessors are still elected. Those not elected are appointed by other politicians. As an appraiser involved in property valuation, I have met many assessors, some knowledgable, some dedicated, practically all unable to do a fair assessment job because of the archaic nature of their job and the political pressures on their work.

Here are a few examples of the political pressures too often implicit in the assessment process:

    1. Pressures on elected and appointed officials from

their political party and from persons who helped them get their jobs.

2. Pressures on assessors to underassess industries which have economic clout.

3. Pressures on assessors to underassess old friends and neighbors; pressures not to raise out-dated values.

4. Pressures on assessors to over-assess newcomers; pressures to up-date values only on sold properties.

5. Pressures to raise assessments rather than politically unpalatable tax rates each year.

The individual taxpayer can always find the one man in this local political process, the assessor, who is responsible legally. The assessor has been barricaded for many years behind this confusing assessing system, protected by compliant administrative appeal boards and by the high legal cost of court review. However, the very same political nature of this assessing game builds into the system so many inconsistencies that a determined, knowledgable taxpayer appellant can usually use these inconsistencies to prosecute a successful tax appeal. This book will continue to show you how to do this.

WHY COMMERICAL AND INDUSTRIAL PROPERTIES ARE OFTEN UNDER-ASSESSED

Assume that your town, a suburb in the economically ailing northeast, is trying to get jobs for its residents. If your state doesn't have laws which permit tax reductions or rebates to industries which locate in it, the local assessor has to do it if he values his job. He will offer and give low assessments to an industry to help it keep its taxes down when it comes to Yourtown. Of course, someone has to pay for the increased municipal services required by the industry, so the residential taxpayer's assessment and taxes are usually raised.

On the other hand, say you live in a city where there are many hundreds of thousands of homeowners (voters) and plenty of industries (not voters). If it is not already sanctioned by law, the assessor usually assesses these different classes of property at a lower rate for residences than for industries.

Whichever way, such differential assessment by classes compounds the inequities in an assessment system becoming more and more unable to handle its job.

TAX EXEMPTIONS CAUSING TAX REBELLION BY TAXPAYERS

Modern property tax rebels don't throw tea into the harbor. In one small rural town in N.Y. they all became ministers by mail ordination and everyone applied for religious tax exemption. This rebellion occurred in reaction to a large increase in these homeowners' property taxes because of tax exemptions given to large parcels recently purchased by charitable, educational and religious institutions which had located in their area.

This instance is a bizarre example of the frustration property owners are experiencing as they see their taxes double and triple and go for broke everywhere. Many states have met this problem of tax exemptions for veteran, educational, religious and other good works institutions by creating even more tax exemptions. Appendix I gives state by state detail on "homestead" and "circuit breaker" exemptions which had to be enacted to provide relief to homeowners through a system of tax credits and rebates whenever property tax payments exceed a certain percentage of family income. One assessment inequity leads to another. Thus, farmers were being driven out of farming because assessors are supposed to value land based on "highest and best use." (See Definitions, Chapter 1 and Appendix Dictionary.) Wherever suburban development was taking place, the farmer saw his assessment and taxes jump ten-fold because land buyers and builders were bidding up land prices in his area. Laws were then passed in many states that farmland be valued based on its farm "use." And on and on and on—this assessment hodge-podge of inequities continues to lurch on towards the 21st century.

ARCHAIC SYSTEM UNABLE TO COPE WITH ITS ASSESSMENT JOB

The root of the problem is the obsolescence of the whole process of real property tax administration. Assessments and taxes are soaring even as we complete these last decades of the 20th century despite efforts to shore up this archaic system with class assessments, tax exemptions and other band-aid measures. Tax-payers are rebelling and voting against community and school budgets everywhere. Higher taxes are driving older people and working people from their homes. In some areas of the country, like economically depressed Long Island, N.Y., high taxes with effective rates of 5% and more of market value are helping to stifle property re-sales and building. Booming areas in the "Sunbelt" areas of our country are putting intense upward pressure on home values and making it difficult for many people to pay rapidly escalating taxes and remain homeowners.

This archaic assessment system does not appear able to respond and change its basic structure, concepts and methods fast enough to cope with these modern challenges. Consumer publications, consumer groups and taxpayer groups have brought some organized but mainly weak pressures to reform the system.

However, the confrontation is still you as an individual versus a system designed by its history, structure and evolution to be unequal. We have noted that the political pressures cause inequities which, if understood, can be used to appeal individual assessments. So too can the very nature of this confusing archaic assessing process be used to appeal individual unequal, unfair assessments which are the usual end product of the process.

WHY 100% REVALUATIONS OFTEN DOUBLE YOUR TAXES

Hundreds, perhaps thousands of mass revaluations of whole communities have been done recently, mainly by private appraisal companies. The theory of this mass updating of values is of course to make all property assessments conform to current value to start off on the right uniform foot. These mass 100% revaluations are usually resorted to locally in desperation because of mounting assessment inaccuracies and complaints. The trouble is, though, that these so called "re-vals" usually wind up compounding rather than solving the problems because of the variety of reasons listed below:

1. Most communities negotiate revaluation contracts with the appraisal companies at so much per property, regardless of its size or complexity. A few years ago, one community paid $10 per parcel at a time when individual appraisals generally cost a minimum of $75 for a home, ranging up to $1000 for large commercial or industrial properties. And $10 worth of work is what that community got. It still hasn't recovered.

2. The appraisal company which is hired sends in a staff to do the job in the community. The number

of experienced appraisers they send depends on what they are being paid. In most communities they hire local people, often students on seasonal vacation, at minimum wages to do the actual field work of listing and describing all properties. The extent of training of these "listers" and the type of data they gather often is sadly inadequate and uninformed.

3. Again, minimal cost of this total assessing job has to be somehow met. Unfortunately again, the old fashioned Cost Approach system is at hand to help do a minimum cost job. Theoretically, the appraisal company's experienced appraisers study the local real estate market, anlayze sales data and descriptions of typical properties (gathered by their inexperienced, "trained" data people), then use this data to establish "bench mark" value tables for all the types of properties in the community. Thus, after these value tables have been designed, each property can then be appraised by checking it for size mainly, type, and features against these tables, assigning its building value and adding land value. This is known as the Cost Approach in appraising. There will be more on this in the later chapters on how to appeal. Enough to say here in introduction that this approach, even when supposedly based locally on the mentioned "bench-mark" value "studies," has not yet resulted in uniform or equal assessment revaluations anywhere. Usually, either the value studies are inadequate or the construction costs used are not local or both sales and costs are not adequate.

4. Even these attempts at uniformity through 100% revaluations are short-lived. By the following year, value and cost changes are throwing the system off again.

5. When your town begins those "re-vals" you usually get a letter which approximately says "Don't worry! We are going to assess at 100%, but if your assessment goes up, your tax rate will go down and your taxes should stay the same." Experience everywhere with "re-vals" has shown that assessments do go up, tax rates stay down only spottily and momentarily and taxes then often double or more. It's true, worry won't help. Understanding and appealing your individual unequal or unfair taxes will.

SOME IMPORTANT COURT DECISIONS AFFECTING YOUR TAXES

Many of these 100% market revaluations have been prompted by various court decisions requiring that assessments be at market value and uniform. Some of the more important decisions in various states including California, New Jersey and New York have struck down lower court rulings that permitted assessors to assess at a percentage of market value and utilize construction cost and Cost Approach rather than market value. In California and New Jersey, courts have also held that state systems of financing schools with property taxes which give richer localities better schools are illegal under state constitutions.

Potentially, the Guth Decision in New York State is probably the most significant insofar as assessment appeals are concerned. Now, state laws everywhere limit assessment tax reductions to the current appeal year with no retroactivity prior to the date appealed. If this New York decision stands and becomes a precedent for spread to other states, it will have an explosive national effect on assessment appeals. This Guth Decision allows property owners to *recoup* taxes they have paid in *prior* years if their appeal proves that the assessment of their property was excessive compared to the average assessment of other properties in their categories. (See Appendix I.)

All these court decisions are affecting assessment procedures and school financing in these states and in other areas also. However, tax assessment is still mainly a "Balkanized" field and knowledge of local assessment practice is still the key for successful tax appeals.

If these introductory chapters have convinced you that the assessment process in our country is mainly in a hopeless, chaotic state, you're right. Also, there are basic questions involving the very nature and structure of this ancient assessment system in our modern society:

1. Should real estate continue to be selectively taxed for current local municipal and school needs?

2. Should other non-real estate assets be taxed instead?

3. How should schools be funded to provide good schools without bankrupting property owners?

4. How can retired persons be protected from losing their homes?

5. How about charitable, educational and religious exemptions?

The winds of change blow ever so slowly. Consumer organizations, taxpayer groups and consumer publications have begun to fight for reform. However, answers to these basic questions and efforts to meet court directed reform appear to be moving slower than glaciers and only in few localities. Oregon has moved into statewide computerized assessment. New York has encouraged some of its communities to accept state-supported computerized assessment assistance. However, this assessment/tax system has survived these hundreds of years with little substantive change. It behooves you to assume it will take a good while longer to really change. It also behooves you to learn how to work within this largely imperfect, unfair system to ensure each year that you are treated at least no more unequal than others.

The succeeding chapters and appendices constitute a plan for translating into action what these beginning chapters have shown you about the system. Simply, you will be given lists of many typical assessment errors and appeal grounds, other detailed help and action plans on how to review your own public property records for unfair assessment, how to informally review with the assessor, how to formally appeal if he turns you down and how to do all you can to reduce your own real estate taxes.

CHAPTER 3

The Reasons for Errors in Your Assessment

The many errors made constantly in assessment become the many reasons for appeal. As the property owner, you are the one most knowledgable about your own property and similar properties in your area. The main working plan of this book is to bring your expertise to bear on this highly imperfect system in order to expose errors in your assessment which then become grounds for appeal to reduce your assessment and taxes.

To this end, this chapter lists many typical errors in assessment. It also groups them in categories which generally correspond to the grounds for appeal permitted in most state regulations. Appendix I gives a 50-state table of Admissible Grounds for appeal so that you can refer to requirements in your area. Because requirements do change, it is also important you check at your assessors or state assessment office for local appeal revisions whenever you begin to review your own public assessment records on your property.

This overall list of assessment errors is generally complete and typical but is not exhaustive. Thorough reviews can pick up additional errors in each category. However, you should not immediately formally or informally appeal merely because a quick review finds a few minor errors. It is important that your review be thorough, systematic and complete in detail for your appeal to be successful. Succeeding chapters will show you how to go about this review and how to follow the appeal procedures in a timely manner. The list of typical errors in this chapter is designed as a categorized, handy reference tool to help you do such systematic reviews. Some fall into the category of arithmetic, recording and judgment errors by the assessor; others into state legal standards regarding overassessment and illegal assessments.

Forty Typical Assessment Errors Become Forty Different Appeal Grounds

The first and most numerous category of errors can be labelled assessment recording errors. This is the broad category which is always your first step in assessment appeal review. Here is when you check the public records to see if the property you own is really the property that has been assessed. Some of the items are major, others minor. It is not only the major errors which count. It's also the cumulative effect of the errors in records you show informally to the assessor or formally to the appeal board which helps get your taxes reduced.

Oregon, the most advanced state in assessment administration, assesses on a statewide basis. It also keeps its records up to date by regularly notifying taxpayers what its records show on their properties and asking the taxpayers to note where there are errors in description. No other localities do this yet, and most public assessment records are wrong in assessment and in detail.

ASSESSMENT RECORD ERRORS

1. *Dimensions of land are wrong.* Check this exactly from your survey or deed description against the assessors property record card.

2. *Dimensions of building(s) are wrong.* This is probably the most important item for description review since most assessors use the square feet of habitable area of buildings to get their values. (See Appendix Dictionary for definitions of square feet, livable area and Cost Approach.) Check measurements carefully from your building plans if you still have them in your files or from actually taking the outside measurements of each level of finished habitable area. (Sometimes, cubic volume of the building is used instead of square feet when the assessor does his computations.)

3. *Description of building is wrong.* Are the building specifications shown on the assessor's record card wrong? Age? Building descriptions? (Example: Does the assessor list your building as masonry when its really frame?)

4. *Description of land is wrong.* Is your plot marked "typical" or "corner" or "level," or "average topography" on the card when it's actually an interior, very steep, rocky lot?

5. *Wrong property assessed.* This has happened.

6. *Arithmetic errors* in land computations.

7. *Arithmetic errors* in building computations.

8. *Depreciating on-site influences* not noted nor completely considered, i.e., wet basements, poor condition, erosion, etc.

9. *Depreciating off-site influences* not noted, i.e., heavy traffic, industrial odors, garbage dump proximity, etc.

10. *Grade and quality of improvements are wrong.* Building and other improvements are rated too high on your property according to the assessors own manual.

11. *Important information omitted from record card.* For example, railroad tracks run close to residence. Property is in a flood area, etc.

12. *Record out-of-date.* For example, the record card still shows a detached garage when it was demolished or fell down 5 years ago.

13. *Finished areas wrong.* Record card might show a finished basement when actually you have a crawl space, or a completed attic when you have a low-pitched roof too low for midgets.

Assessments Higher than Legal Standard

(This "Higher than Legal Standard" category includes overassessments which specifically violate your state's assessments laws. This is so regardless of whether your state requires "full cash value" assessments, "true cash value" assessments, "fair market value" assessments, "100% market value" assessments (all meaning the same really—current market value.) This is also so even if your state legally specifies a percentage rather than full current market values. (See appendix I for "Admissible Appeal Grounds" and "Full and Partial Value" data.)

14. *Property overassessed at more than market value* in states which require that assessments be at current market value.

15. *Property overassessed at more than legal percentage* in states which require that assessments be at percentage of current market value.

16. *Higher than legal standard for class of property.* For example, your home might be assessed at 70% of current market value when your state requires by law that assessments on residences are not to exceed 55% of current market value. Or you may own commercial property which is supposed to be assessed at 70% of current market value and it's been assessed at 90%.

ASSESSMENTS HIGHER THAN SIMILAR PROPERTIES

(This category deals with the most frequent overassessment: "Higher than Similar . . ." category. This is a category which should be carefully checked. It is critical to most appeals.) (See also Appendix I.)

17. *Assessments on similar properties lower.* Correspondingly, this category also includes overassessments when compared to better properties which are assessed equal to or lower than yours. You know your property and area. This is where you can best use your knowledge to review, compare and appeal.

ASSESSMENTS HIGHER THAN LEGAL AVERAGE FOR DISTRICT

(This category is specific to assessments which are higher than "Legal Average for District." In this connection, see Appendix I, Admissible Grounds and Partial/Full Value, as well as Appendix III, Dictionary on "Assessment-Sales Ratio."

18. *State issued sales-assessment ratio* percentage (sometimes called equalization ratio), shows your assessment is higher than this ratio.

19. *Your own sales-assessment ratio study* of say 25 recently sold similar properties shows your assessment is higher than the percentage you derived.

Miscellaneous Assessment Errors

(This miscellaneous category is a catch-all for all errors which do not fall into the preceding groupings.)

20. *Property in wrong class.* Because of zoning or usage or design, property is actually in one class and overassessed as another. For example, your property might be classified as commercial and assessed at higher commercial percentage, even though it is barred by zoning or deed restrictions from commercial use.

21. *Assessment illegal.* There can be numerous examples depending on each state's laws. A few: Assessor failed to inspect property before raising assessment even though the law requires exterior and interior inspection; Assessor used one approach to value when state manual requires another, etc.

22. *Property not in assessment district.* Particularly in rural and exurban areas where tax maps are not available, this should be carefully checked if property is near political boundaries.

23. *Personal property in real estate assessed.* Personal property like kitchen appliances, washers, dryers included by assessor but legally exempt as non-real estate property.

24. *No notice of increased assessment issued or received.* This often happens and by itself would not be a strong ground for appeal. However, added to the weight of other errors, it can correspondingly add to the weight of the appeal evidence.

25. *Property recently purchased for less than appraised value.* This is a good, strong argument for assessment reduction.

26. *Maintenance items used to increase assessments.* Maintenance items like re-roofing and painting used by as-

sessor to increase assessments rather than actual additions or major remodellings like porches or upgraded kitchens or baths.

27. *Income Approach used in error.* Income Approach used by assessor on say, apartment buildings based on an erroneous rent schedule.

28. *Standard cost manual improperly used.* If state mandates that assessors use a standard cost manual, such as Marshall & Stevens', has it been properly used to value the property?

29. *Depreciation allowances in error.* Has enough percentage of depreciation been deducted from the property's replacement cost in accordance with the required state or other manual?

30. *Highest and best use.* (See Appendix III, Dictionary, for "highest and best use" definition.) Your property may have been given an incorrect highest and best use. For example, zoning and usage may have changed and property is still assessed at commercial higher use when it should be lowered in assessment to present legal lower assessed industrial use.

31. *Higher than construction cost.* Property assessed for more than recent construction cost, if new.

32. *Shoddy construction.* Property not depreciated for shoddy construction if recently built and/or, for example, if suffering from chronic construction defects, such as water in the basement, etc.

33. *Electric heat.* With today's high energy costs, property overassessed because it has electric heat and is therefore less marketable and less valuable than houses with other heat, particularly in northern sections of our country.

34. *Exemptions.* Property overassessed because it is entitled to partial or full exemption because of its use

or ownership. (See later complete list and Appendix I.)

35. *Environmental restrictions.* Property overassessed because environmental, planning board, or state control regulations prohibit its improvement. (For example, wetlands, flood plains, etc.)

36. *"Use" assessments.* Property overassessed because it is legally entitled to a reduced "use" assessment (i.e. farmland, in many states.)

37. *Restrictive covenants.* Property overassessed because restrictions in the deed bar it from its highest and best use (i.e., land on a prime commercial corner barred by deed covenant from being used except as a residence).

38. *Lack of utilities.* Property overassessed because impermeable soil and no available water bar its improvement in an area beyond public water and sewer mains.

39. *Veterans.* Many states grant partial exemption to veterans, disabled veterans and veterans' widows. It is not automatic. Application must be made or property will continue to be over-taxed.

40. *Easements.* Property overassessed because a high voltage utility line overhead or other recorded restrictive easement prohibits or limits building or use of part or all of the property.

CHAPTER 4

How to Research an Appeal

The prior chapters covered how you are assessed and why your assessment can be wrong in so many ways. This is the part of the book which guides you on researching your own assessment. This is where you use what you have learned about this archaic assessment system with its built-in inequities to find your way through the system to lower your own real estate taxes. This chapter gives specific direction on how to review all the public facts on your assessment. There is a section here also on how to read the assessors property tax card on your property. A companion section shows how to compare your property deed description to the assessors land description and/or tax map. Finally, to help you prepare for your appeal, there is a construction and site influence checklist to use on your own property to determine those items which subtract from the value of your property.

How You Do the Appeal Research

Most assessor offices use similar record-keeping procedures. These records are public and available for inspections by appointment or other appropriate arrangements.

Before you start your research, review how your property is assessed and taxed as summarized below: (See also Chapters 1 and 2.)

Phase 1—Listing of Properties. The assessor in your district each year lists your property along with all the other properties in the taxing district. This is a continuous process; he does it throughout the year, adding newly built properties, listing changes in properties, additions and demolitions.

Phase 2—Tax roll. Once a year, the assessor assesses all the properties in the district and issues all these assessment valuations in a complete tax roll which is announced, published or posted for public review. During this period of public announcement, the roll is usually "tentative." This period usually also coincides with the "grievance" or appeal period in most states. It is during this time that taxpayers can formally "grieve" or complain for changes or reductions in their assessments, before they become final.

Phase 3—Tax Bill. After this "grievance" period, the roll becomes final, is turned over to the tax collector who then sends you a tax bill for payment.

It is important that you find out from your assessor these dates for your own area. Of course, you can do your own investigation and research anytime during the year on your own assessment records and on similar neighboring properties. You can also informally discuss your complaint and request informal review by the assessor anytime during the year. However, it is critical to know that in practically all localities, changes, corrections, additions and deletions to property assessments can only be made once each year when the tax roll is established. Similarly, you must file your formal appeal prior to the end of the formal "grievance" or complaint period. If you wait until you get your tax bill, it's already legally too late. Your complaint for reduction would have to wait until next year.

Before you begin your research, you should also know the bases for most appeals, which generally fall into the following broad categories:

Category 1—Illegal Assessment. For example, your property might be outside the taxing district or should be exempt partially or fully.

Category 2—Assessment in error. For example, plot size is incorrect or improvements like size of building or what's in it or how it's constructed may be in error.

Category 3—Assessment not equal. For example, your rate of assessment is higher than the average rate of assessment in your district, or higher than a good number of similar properties in your neighborhood, or higher than market value in those states which require full market value assessments.

You should also know how the assessor applies assessment rates if your property is in an area which does permit by law or in practice less than full value assessments. (Most areas in this country are in this category.) The assessor multiplies the market value of the property by the assessment rate to get the assessment. Thus, if the assessor determines your property is worth $50,000 in today's market and the assessment rate is 60%, then the following arithmetic would apply:

$$\$50,000 \times 60\% = \$30,000 \text{ Assessment}$$

The assessor can tell you how much the assessment rate is. It is important that you check out for yourself at what rate your property is actually being assessed when compared to its current market value. In most areas, this actual rate is far from the legal or average rate the assessor says he is using. To do this checking, you follow the below-listed procedure:

Step 1—Determine market value. Find out what your property is worth now from the following sources:

    (a) *Construction cost*, plus land value, if recently built.

    (b) *Purchase price*, if recently bought.

    (c) *Professional appraisal* of your property.

    (d) *Recent comparable sales* of similar properties.

    (e) *Capitalization of net income*, if commercial or industrial or other income producing property.

    (f) *Offering prices* of your property and similar properties, if recently put on market for sale.

Step 2—Determine your assessment rate. From Step 1, take market value, then divide market value into the assessment of your property (usually shown on your tax bill) to get the assessment rate on your own property.

Step 3—Compare assessment rates. Compare the rate you have derived to the average or legal rate given you by the assessor. If there is more than a 5% difference, go on to the next step.

Step 4—Secure actual average rate. There are several approaches:

    (a) Make a list of 25 similar properties in your area which have sold recently, together with their assessments at time of sale. You can get such lists of sales from brokers or the loan officer in your bank. You can get the assessments for these sold properties from the assessor's records. Do the arithmetic to get the average assessment-sales ratio.

(b) Some states will give you an average assessment-sales ratio for your district. (See Appendix II, State Data Sources.)

(c) Compare the assessment of similar houses in your locality to your own. Is yours higher than the average? This is particularly pertinent in an area of similar suburban development type homes, built from the same models about the same time.

How to Review Your Own Assessment Property Record Card

The object of the preceding background data is to give you an understanding of what goes into the making of your assessment and what you have to do to see that you pay no more than your fair share. With this background, you can then begin the below listed actual research procedure:

First Step—Visit assessor. Call assessor's office to make an appointment. Go there and ask to see the assessment card on your property. It is a public record and open for your inspection when the office is open to public business, if arranged for properly.

Second Step—Review of description on property card. Review card thoroughly for errors in description. (See Chapter 5 for detailed review of possible errors.) If you can, try to arrange to get a duplicate copy of the card from the assessor. Offer to pay for the duplication. If you go on to appeal later to a higher board, this may be important evidence. If you cannot get a duplicate, copy down all important information, particularly incorrect items.

Third Step—Computation review of property card. Since the assessment is usually based on the Cost Approach, check all computations carefully for correct arithmetic.

Fourth Step—Neighbors' property cards review. Review the public record property cards for as many similar properties in your neighborhood that you can identify. This is to determine if there are assessment inequities in your property compared to your neighbors who have similar properties. Note that many areas now have tax maps, and tax rolls in such areas are usually by Section, Block and Lot or similar legal designation rather than by street or postal address. Assessor offices also have index books by name of owner or tax maps by location which give these legal designations. You can ask for these index type records to identify and get your neighbors' property cards. You probably will be asked to trace these numbers yourself through these indexing books or maps. It is not difficult. These are also public records open to you as a taxpayer in the district.

Fifth Step—Consult with assessor. If incorrect data is found on the assessors cards on your property or when compared to your neighbors' similar properties (and there are few perfect assessment cards), take this information to the assessor. At this appeal stage, you are dealing with public facts on record, not opinions. If there are substantial errors of fact, the assessor has the authority to correct these errors and change assessments at this preliminary stage of your appeal when he later prepares the tax roll for the year.

Sixth Step—Check assessment rate. If descriptions and computations are correct or if assessor does not agree that errors warrant a substantial reduction, then go on to this assessment rate review. If there is a legal assessment rate in your state, then the card may have that percentage stated in the computations. Even if not, it is most important that you check this rate which is defined as the percentage of the full value of your property at which it is assessed. In order to determine the actual rate of assessment on your property, divide the market value of your property into the assessed value. If the resultant rate is, for example, 50% and is more than the average 40% rate of assessment for other similar properties and/or for the district, then you have a complaint of inequity.

Securing lists of properties which have sold and comparing them to their assessed value can take time but may well be worth your while. Reviewing the assessments of similar unsold properties can also be a good method of determining inequity. Do not be turned off in your review by an assessor's offhand observation that "You can get much more for your property than it's assessed," or "If you appeal, we might raise up your assessment to what it's worth." These are often-used ploys to avoid or defuse appeals. The important thing in practically all areas is the rate at which the property is assessed, whether it is legal or equal and fair. Practically all assessments by the nature of this sytem, are not at market value.

A sample Orange County, N.Y., Property Record card is used in the following Chapter 5 to illustrate on a practical basis what has been given in this review procedure. The prior Chapter 3 also has a catalogue of 40 common errors found in public property assessment records.

HOW TO COMPARE YOUR PROPERTY DEED DESCRIPTION TO ASSESSORS RECORDS

All value stems from the land. Location, location, location are the three bases for land value. These and similar appraisal sayings demonstrate how important the land and its location is to property value and assessment. This land check, together with your review of the assessor's total square feet of habitable area of your building improvements, are probably the two most important parts of your preliminary assessment property card review.

If the dimensions of your land are incorrect, if the road frontage is mis-stated, if the wrong land has been assessed, all these and more are grounds for appeal based on improper land assessment. This land phase of the assessment process is so important that practically all public record cards show one value for building improvements and a separate value for land before combining them into a total assessment.

Your procedure for comparing your legal deed description to the assessor's property land description is as follows:

Step 1—Review your deed description. Every property owner has a deed which was given to him by the former owner when purchased. This deed describes the land, not the building improvements. It can be in a number of different forms. Some deeds describe the land by stating the beginning point of one corner as a distance and in a direction from the nearest road intersection, then reciting all boundaries and directions of the plot. For example: "Beginning 100' south of the northwest corner of Elm Street and Maple Street on the west side of Elm Street, then running 80' south ___ degrees, then 150' west ___ degrees, then 80' north ___ degrees along Elm Street to the point and place of beginning."

The above is called a metes and bounds description. A recorded copy is in the public records, usually in the county clerk's office. Other descriptions may refer to your property as a section and a lot number on a map on file in the county clerk's office. Thus:

". . . known as Section 3, Lot 2 of Map of Evergreen Knolls, on file in County Clerks office, Yourtown, U.S.A."

Whatever the form, wherever you find it, either among your own important records or as a copy or map in the county clerk's office, you review it carefully for road frontage, depth, dimensions, total square feet or acreage and location in relation to its adjoining properties.

Step 2—Review property card land description. The assessor's card will usually have road frontage, depth, dimensions, square feet of land and/or acreage as well as location information by names of neighbors or adjoining roads. Compare this all carefully to your own legal deed information.

Step 3—Check assessors land computations. Many assessors compute and assign land values based on "effective," (usable) road frontage and depth dimensions. This is a judgment decision. You know your property best. The assessor may have recorded that you have 80′ "effective" frontage and 100′ "effective" depth out of a 100′×150′ plot. You live on the plot though and know and should be able to prove to him that there is only one knoll which is not too steep to be usable and the plot should really be valued at 50′ effective frontage × 60′ effective depth. This is but one example. You may have or be able to get personal knowledge of sales of similar lots nearby at less than he has valued your land. Or you may find that he has valued your neighbors similar plots at less, etc., etc.

So long as most assessors continue to value improved properties by the Cost Approach with separate values for land, this review of land value assessments will be one of your more important appeal steps.

A Construction and Site Influence Checklist to Use on Your Property

You not only have to thoroughly review the assessors records on your property; you have to know every detail of your property in its location to be able to compare it to its public description. You also have to be aware of the items which you believe subtract from the value of your property. The assessor may not know from his inspections or from his records that you have a chronic wet basement, that you still have galvanized plumbing which needs constant maintenance, that your building doesn't have minimum 100 Amp electric service, that erosion is a constant problem, that deed restrictions limit its use or expansion of use upon which the assessment was based. These are but a few examples of components of a property which affect and detract from value and which can be used in your assessment review and appeal.

The following Construction and Site Influence Checklist is a handy guide for this review:

CONSTRUCTION AND SITE INFLUENCE CHECKLIST

THE SITE

___ Access to property safe, maintained?

___ Heavy, fast traffic?

___ Community facilities, transportation, schools convenient?

___ Is area flood prone?

___ Any inharmonious nearby usages? For example, in residential areas, nearby uses which cause odors, smoke, noise, traffic, unsightly views?

___ Are all building improvements within lot? Any encroachments?

___ Does block and lot drain properly? Any ponding?

___ Does lot need fill? Any subsidence?

___ Are yard areas usable? Do grades permit access and function?

___ Does zoning permit usage? Do deed restrictions bar any use?

___ Any erosion? Are soils stable?

___ Septic system problems? Adequate well yield?

___ Landscaping appropriate?

BUILDING INTERIOR

___ Layout functional?

___ Size of rooms and halls adequate for function and clearance?

___ Adequate storage for exterior items?

___ Commensurate kitchen, if residence?

_____ Enough windows which work properly?

_____ Enough electric service and outlets?

_____ Enough insulation in ceiling & walls, storm windows?

_____ Plaster or drywall free of excessive cracks or nailpops?

_____ Acceptable floor and wall finishes?

_____ Plumbing working properly?

_____ Ceiling leaks (evidencing roof or plumbing problem)?

_____ Adequate, balanced heat?

_____ Fireplace works without hazard?

BASEMENT OR CRAWL SPACE

_____ Settlement? Is basement floor serviceable?

_____ If sump pump is involved, does it discharge properly so the effluent won't come back into basement?

_____ Condition of plumbing?

_____ Was basement dug out deeper after house built on crawl foundation? Were footings undermined? Are all walls plumb? No structural wall failures?

_____ Termite tubes? Termite damage?

_____ Dry rot in framing members?

_____ Is there floor insulation in electric heated houses?

_____ Less than 18″ clearance in crawl space?

_____ Does crawl space have vents? Is it dry?

_____ Are crawl openings big enough for inspection and maintenance?

MISCELLANEOUS

_____ Are plumbing pipes insulated in built-in or attached garages?

____ Is heating unit firewalled from built-in garage area?

____ Is garage long enough for cars?

____ Firewall on common wall of attached garage?

____ Enough insulation in built-in garage ceiling and in common wall of attached garage?

____ Pool and all necessary equipment serviceable?

CHAPTER 5

How to Check for Errors in Assessor's Records on Your Property

This chapter completes the trilogy of chapters on assessment errors. It gives specific detail on how to locate errors in these public records to help you get a tax reduction. The first section in this chapter provides a checklist of land errors in assessment records. Subsequent sections emphasize building description errors and errors in neighborhood "ratings." Identifying arithmetic errors is also particularly stressed since assessment is basically a Cost Approach numerical valuation system. Guidance is then provided on the ever-present assessment problem involving failure to assess similar properties uniformly. Finally, a sample model assessment property card is checked for errors.

ERRORS IN LAND DESCRIPTION

The following checklist of possible errors in land description can be used when you check the assessor's card for over-valuation or improper assessment of land on your property:

ASSESSMENT LAND ERRORS CHECKLIST

_____ *Wrong property*—Property on the card is not your land.

_____ *Wrong dimensions*—There is less road frontage or less total square feet or acreage.

_____ *Incorrect Description*—Property is not a corner as described on cards or not level as shown under topography.

_____ *Not in taxing district*—The property is partly or entirely over the boundary line of this taxing district and in another community.

_____ *Wrong classification*—Land is classed as commercial when it is actually zoned residential.

_____ *Outdated description*—Listed and valued as residential even though part or all of the building improvements burned down or were demolished long ago.

_____ *Errors in influence*—For example, coded and valued for "view" when actually the property is level and physically separated from any view by unaesthetic buildings.

_____ *Incomplete data*—Even though the assessor received a copy of the deed, he did not, for example, note that the land has deed restrictions against any commercial usage when he valued the land as commercial property.

_____ *Calculations wrong*—Front-foot price, depth factors,

frontage or any land arithmetic on property card is in error and substantially affects the assessment.

ERRORS IN BUILDING DESCRIPTION

This is where most errors are found on assessment property records and where most of the value is assigned on the vast majority of improved properties. It pays the taxpayer to spend his time carefully in this phase, completely familiarizing himself with the details of his own building(s) and locating any and all discrepancies on the assessment building(s) description records. Practically all assessors use the Cost Approach system to value properties. This system involves describing, measuring, classifying and grading building improvements, then multiplying the square or cubic feet of the building by a dollar rate amount taken from a cost manual to arrive at replacement cost, new, for the building. This replacement figure is defined as how much it would theoretically cost to rebuild the building now with similar materials. Depreciation is then taken. In other words, the replacement cost is depreciated or lessened by judgment percentage amounts deducted for physical age, normal wear and tear, functional items like layout and old facilities, and for economic or adverse influences in the vicinity.

This whole careful mathematical procedure can be sent tumbling on assessment appeal if its foundation, the building description, can be shown to be partly or wholly wrong in specification. Such discrepancies can also be used when comparing the assessment on similar properties if these errors have caused overvaluation on your property. The following "Errors in Building Description" Checklist is a handy tool for this assessment appeal research:

CHECKLIST OF ERRORS
IN BUILDING DESCRIPTION

____ *Building components wrong*—The assessment card does not describe the buildings correctly. Examples follow:

____ *Exterior walls*—Assessor's card says "brick veneer." Side and rear walls are actually asbestos shingles.

____ *Foundation*—Property card shows "poured concrete, full basement." Building is actually concrete block, 50% basement.

____ *Roof*—"Slate shingles" on card; asphalt shingles on roof.

____ *Floors*—Card says "hardwood." Floor is old carpet over plywood.

____ *Interior finish*—Baths shown as "ceramic"; only tile in bath is plastic and that at tub only.

____ *Fireplace*—"Fireplace" listed; none in house.

____ *Electric*—Card says "adequate"; actually inadequate 60 Amp.

____ *Other*—Card shows "enclosed porch"; porch is open.

____ *Year built is incorrect*—Age of building is wrong.

____ *Construction grade wrong*—For example, marked "good" when actually building should be less than average because of water in basement, leaking roof, etc.

____ *Dimensions of building wrong*—Wrong in part or whole. Important.

____ *Number of stories wrong*—Marked as a 2-story house, say, when actually it is one-story with partly finished below-grade basement. (This affects amount of livable square feet.)

____ *Overall description incorrect*—Card identifies building as a 3-family type when actually it is a 2-family dwelling.

ERRORS IN NEIGHBORHOOD RATINGS

Many assessor's cards rate neighborhood desirability on a rating scale ranging from excellent through very good, good, average, fair, poor to very poor. Topography and landscaping are usually rated from good to very poor. Your lot is often rated on the assessor's card as typical to its surroundings, better or poorer. Other residential property factors such as zoning, type of road paving, sidewalks, utilities, driveway and traffic are described. The neighborhood type is also often classified as rural, urban, suburban or subdivision.

Since every one of the above ratings characterize and affect the value of your property, it behooves you to carefully review your property card for any discrepancies in these ratings. You are the one most familiar with your neighborhood. True, these are all judgment factors and there may be a difference of opinion between you and the assessor. However, you might be able to show that an important factor such as neighborhood desirability is deteriorating because of say, much heavier, noisier traffic. Or landscaping is marked as very good when there are no shrubs or trees, or driveway is shown paved when there is no paving.

ARITHMETIC ERRORS

To err is human and assessors are human. They are also usually overworked, underpaid and in most cases not qualified. (See Appendix I which shows that most states have neither experience nor education requirements for assessors.) With the best of intentions, the average assessor has to cope with overwhelming data on many thousands of different properties in his district. It is rare indeed to find fully described records. It is equally rare to find all computations pertinent and correct.

Practically all assessments are made using the Cost Approach system. Even if the square foot of the house has been "taken off" correctly, if the correct dollar factor has been chosen as a multiplier for the square feet, if proper percentages of physical, functional and economic depreciation have been deducted, the arithmetic is usually found wanting in this very "iffy" archaic mumbo-jumbo numbers game. Bring your pocket calculator. Check all the arithmetic carefully.

Assessor's Failure to Assess Uniformly

More and more state courts are ruling that 100% market value assessment is required. A few states like Oregon with the help of sophisticated computer systems are trying to do this. Most don't, and even when they try for a while, usually backslide soon to a percentage of less than market value.

"So what if we're not at 100%," say the systems apologists, "so long as we're uniform. If we assess at ½% or 50% of value, what difference so long as its uniform."

This rationalization sounds good in theory, but in real assessment life it just simply is not true. Poor administration, poor current market data, politics and untrained often overburdened personnel cause inequities everywhere. Not only do inequities abound between districts but often even between classes of properties in the same district. Commercial-industrial properties are often under-assessed deliberately in one community compared to residential properties, and vice-versa in another community. Politics, the desire to get re-elected, is often many times more influential on the assessor than equity. Tax exemptions given to religious and educational properties are a burden to individual taxpayers. Agricultural, forest lands and other specially reduced assessment districts further reduce total ratables in many districts requiring more tax money (often through higher assessments as well as through higher tax rates) from the remaining taxpayers.

As an individual, you can of course join with taxpayer groups, consumer groups and other groups trying to reform this ancient inequitable system. Reform will no doubt take a long time. Meanwhile, it would be worthwhile on an individual basis to do the necessary research to make sure that as an individual citizen taxpayer, you are being assessed no more unfairly than similar properties.

To this end, you should also make a list at the assessor's office of all the assessments of properties you believe are similar to yours. A simple worksheet describing your property and each of the compared properties and their assessments will take some of your research time but is the right way to seek errors in uniformity of assessment. (See Chapter 8 for details and for sample worksheet.)

A Sample Orange County, N.Y. Record Card

The following card is used in Orange County, N.Y., and is a good example of assessor's public record cards on properties. Review this important record carefully when you check your own property card. This is where your tax bill starts.

Property record cards like the Residential/Farm/Vacant

Data Collection form should always be carefully scruti-nized for accuracy. Basic categories of review questions follow:

1. Are the land computations correct?
2. Does the card have land description which com-pares properly with your deed description?
3. Does your property actually have the paved streets and sidewalks which are shown on the record?
4. Has there been recent decline in the "excellent" neighborhood rating shown?
5. Are all depreciating on-site and off-site influences included?
6. Are the building specifications correctly described?
7. Was building measured correctly?
8. Square feet of livable area correct?
9. Grade of improvements correct?

PROPERTY CLASSIFICATION CODES

AGRICULTURE—100
105—Agricultural Vacant Land
110—Livestock & Products
   111—Poultry & Products
   112—Dairy & Products
   113—Cattle, Hogs & Prod.
   114—Sheep & Wool
   115—Honey & Beeswax
   116—Other Livestock
120—Field Crops
130—Truck Crops/Muckland
140—Truck Crops
150—Orchard Crops
   151—Tree Fruits
   152—Vineyards
160—Other Fruits
170—Nursery/Greenhouse
181—Fur Products
182—Pheasant
183—Aquatic
190—Fish/Game/Wildlife

RESIDENTIAL—200
210—1 Family Year-Round
220—2 Family Year-Round
230—3 Family Year-Round
240—Rural Residence with
   Acreage
250—Estate
260—Seasonal Residence
270—Mobile Home

VACANT LAND—300
311—Residential Vacant
312—Residential Vacant,
   Improved
313—Waterfront Vacant
314—Rural, 10 Acres or Less
321—Abandon Agricultural
322—Rural Res. 10 Ac. or More
323—Other Rural Vacant
330—Commercial Vacant
340—Industrial Vacant
350—Urban Renewal

COMMERCIAL—400
411—Apartments
417—Camps, Cottages (Rental)
418—Inns/Lodges/Boarding
439—SmallParking Garage
483—Partial Residential Use

WILD & FORESTED—900
910—Private (except 920)
920—Private Hunting & Fishing
930—State Owned
940—County Owned

*Consult detailed listing for
further divisions as applicable

MEMORANDA

	19___	19___
ASSESSMENT		
LAND		
IMPROVEMENTS		
TOTAL		
EXEMPTION		
TAXABLE		

DWG. COMPUTATIONS

BASE PRICE	
PLUMBING	
BASEMENT	
BSMT. FINISH	
ATTIC	
HEATING	
OTHER FEATURES	
ADDITIONS	
TOTAL BASE	
GRADE FACTOR	
TOTAL	
C & D FACTOR	
REPL. COST	
DEPRECIATION	%
BLDG. VALUE	

CARD ____ OF ____

LAND DESCRIPTION 3	VALUATION FRONTAGE	VALUATION DEPTH	UNIT PRICE	DEPTH FACTOR	ADJUSTED FF PRICE	INFLUENCE CODE ±	LAND VALUE
0 NONE N							

LAND CODES   LOT
01 PRIMARY SITE
02 SECONDARY SITE
03 UNDEVELOPED
04 RESIDUAL
05 TILLABLE
06 PASTURE   SQUARE
07 WOODLAND   FEET
08 WASTELAND
09 MUCK
10 WATERFRONT
11 ORCHARD
12 REAR
13 HOMESITE   ACREAGE
14 APARTMENT SITE
15 PROPOSED ROAD
16 R.O.W.
17 OTHER

SQ. FT
SQ. FT
SQ. FT
SQ. FT
ACRES
ACRES
ACRES
ACRES
ACRES
ACRES

INFLUENCE CODES
1 CORNER
2 TOPOGRAPHY
3 UNIMPROVED
4 EXCESSIVE FRONT
5 SHAPE OR SIZE
6 RESTRICTIONS
7 ECONOMIC
   MISIMPROVED
8 VIEW
0 NONE

SITE VALUE
01 SITE VALUE   V

RECORD OF OWNERSHIP

1
2
3
4
5

SPECIAL DISTRICTS

SEWER	FIRE
PARK	WATER
SCHOOL	LIGHT

AUDIT CONTROL

MEASURED BY: ____ DATE __ __ __

LISTED BY ____ DATE __ __ __

SOURCE: 1 OWNER 2 SPOUSE 3 TENANT
          4 OTHER 5 ESTIMATE 6 REFUSAL

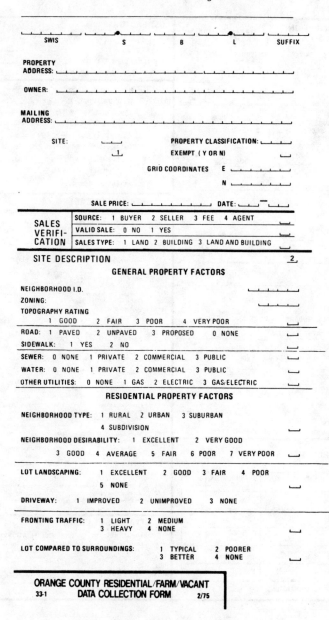

SWIS   S   B   L   SUFFIX

PROPERTY
ADDRESS:

OWNER:

MAILING
ADDRESS:

SITE: PROPERTY CLASSIFICATION:
                    1   EXEMPT (Y OR N)

                         GRID COORDINATES   E

                                             N

                    SALE PRICE: DATE:

SALES   SOURCE: 1 BUYER 2 SELLER 3 FEE 4 AGENT
VERIFI-   VALID SALE: 0 NO 1 YES
CATION   SALES TYPE: 1 LAND 2 BUILDING 3 LAND AND BUILDING

SITE DESCRIPTION   2

GENERAL PROPERTY FACTORS

NEIGHBORHOOD I.D.
ZONING:
TOPOGRAPHY RATING
      1 GOOD   2 FAIR   3 POOR   4 VERY POOR
ROAD: 1 PAVED   2 UNPAVED   3 PROPOSED   0 NONE
SIDEWALK: 1 YES   2 NO
SEWER: 0 NONE   1 PRIVATE   2 COMMERCIAL   3 PUBLIC
WATER: 0 NONE   1 PRIVATE   2 COMMERCIAL   3 PUBLIC
OTHER UTILITIES: 0 NONE   1 GAS   2 ELECTRIC   3 GAS/ELECTRIC

RESIDENTIAL PROPERTY FACTORS

NEIGHBORHOOD TYPE: 1 RURAL 2 URBAN   3 SUBURBAN
                    4 SUBDIVISION
NEIGHBORHOOD DESIRABILITY: 1 EXCELLENT   2 VERY GOOD
      3 GOOD   4 AVERAGE   5 FAIR   6 POOR   7 VERY POOR

LOT LANDSCAPING: 1 EXCELLENT   2 GOOD 3 FAIR   4 POOR
                     5 NONE
DRIVEWAY: 1 IMPROVED   2 UNIMPROVED   3 NONE

FRONTING TRAFFIC: 1 LIGHT   2 MEDIUM
                     3 HEAVY   4 NONE

LOT COMPARED TO SURROUNDINGS: 1 TYPICAL   2 POORER
                                  3 BETTER   4 NONE

ORANGE COUNTY RESIDENTIAL/FARM/VACANT
33-1   DATA COLLECTION FORM   2/75

RESIDENCE DESCRIPTION [4]

STYLE:

01 BI-LEVEL	05 COLONIAL	09 CONVT'L
02 SPLIT-LEVEL	06 CONTEMPORY	10 MANSION
03 RANCH	07 ROW TYPE	11 COTTAGE
04 CAPE COD	08 OLD STYLE	12 OTHER

NUMBER OF STORIES: .●

EXTERIOR WALLS:

1 BRICK	4 CONC BLK	7 STONE
2 FRAME	5 STUCCO	8 METAL, VINYL
3 BR & FR	6 TILE	9 CONCRETE

AGE: YEAR BUILT 1____ REMODELED 1____

ROOMS: BED____ BATH ● FAMILY ____

TOTAL ____

BASEMENT:
1 PIERS/SLAB 2 CRAWL 3 PART 4 FULL ____

FINISHED AREA (SF) ____

ONE CAR OPENINGS ____ TWO CAR OPENINGS ____

HEATING: 0 NONE 1 INADEQUATE 2 ADEQUATE ____

AIR CONDITIONING: 0 NO 1 YES ____

PLUMBING: 0 NO 1 YES ____

NUMBER OF KITCHENS: ____

STYLE OF KITCHENS:
0 NONE 1 OLD 2 SEMI-MODERN 3 MODERN ____

KITCHEN QUALITY (SEE BATH QL. CODES) ____

BATH 0 NONE 2 GOOD 4 ECONOMY
QUALITY 1 EXPENSIVE 3 AVERAGE 5 INEXPENSIVE ____

OTHER FACTORS:
MASONRY TRIM (SF) ____ FIREPLACES ____

INTERIOR CONDITION ____

EXTERIOR CONDITION ____

RELATIVE DESIRABILITY ____
0 UNINHABITABLE 1 GOOD 2 AVERAGE 3 FAIR 4 POOR

ATTACHED IMPROVEMENTS [6]

	STR. CODE	MOD. CODE	U *	MEASUREMENT 1	MEASUREMENT 2	QUAN-TITY
1						
2						
3						
4						
5						

* UNITS 1 QUANTITY 2 DIMENSIONS 3 SQUARE FEET

COST FACTORS [5]

GRADE: ** ____ GRADE ADJ ____ ± %

PERCENT GOOD ____ %

FUNCTIONAL DEPRECIATION ____ %

CDU (EX, VG, G_, AV, F_, P_, VP, UN) ____

LIVING AREA

FIRST FLOOR (SF)	____
SECOND FLOOR (SF)	____
ADDITIONAL FLOOR (SF)	____
HALF STORY FINISHED (SF)	____
HALF STORY UNFINISHED (SF)	____
TOTAL LIVING AREA (SF)	____
UNFINISHED ROOM (SF)	____
FINISHED ATTIC (SF)	____
RECREATION ROOM (SF)	____

DETACHMENT CODES

	STRUCTURES		MODIFICATIONS
RG4	1 Story Detached Garage	I02	Finished Room
RG5	1.5 Story Detached Garage		Area in Garage
RG6	2 Story Detached Garage		
RM5	Mobile Home (Dimensions)	I06	7 x 12 Addition (Quantity)
LP1	Concrete Paving	I07	7 x 24 Addition
LP4	Asphalt Paving		(Quantity)
LS1	Steel Vinyl Lined Inground Pool	H03	Electric Heater (Quantity)
LS2	Concrete, Gunite or Fiberglas Inground Pool	H10	Gas or Propane Heater (Quantity)
LS5	Above Ground Pool		
MS1	Miscellaneous Structure (Dollars)		
FB1	1 Story Dairy Barn	I01	Milk House
FB2	1.5 Story Dairy Barn	I02	Milking Parlor
FB3	2 Story Dairy Barn	I03	Stalls (Quantity)
FB4	1 Story Gen. Pr. Barn	S03	Multiple Section
FB5	1.5 Story Gen. Pr. Barn		(Quantity)
FB6	2 Story Gen. Pr. Barn		
FB7	Pole Barn		
FB8	Horse Barn		
FM1	Milk House	I03	Stalls (Quantity)
FM2	Milking Parlor		
FS1	Concrete Stave Silo	R03	No Roof (Quantity)
FS2	Harvestore Silo	E04	Bottom Unloader
FS3	Wood Stave Silo		(Quantity)
FS4	Tile or Block Silo		Neither Modification
FS5	Metal Silo		Applies to FS2
FC1	Machinery Shed	B06	Concrete Floor
FC2	Aluminum Shed	L01	Electricity
FC3	Galvanized Shed	H06	Central Heat
FC4	Finished Metal Shed		
FQ5	Quonset Shed	H06	Central Heat
		L02	No Electricity
		B03	Earth Floor
FP1	1 Story Poultry House	W07	Masonry Walls
FP2	2 Story Poultry House		(Quantity)
FP3	Additional Story	H09	Ventilation
		H07	No Insulation

ATTACHMENT CODES

	STRUCTURES		MODIFICATIONS
RP1	Open Porch	S05	Second Story
RP2	Covered Porch		Porch Area
RP4	Enclosed Porch		(Quantity)
RC1	Carport		
RG1	1 Story Attached Garage	I02	Finished Room
RG2	1.5 Story Attached Garage		Area in Garage
RG3	2 Story Attached Garage		

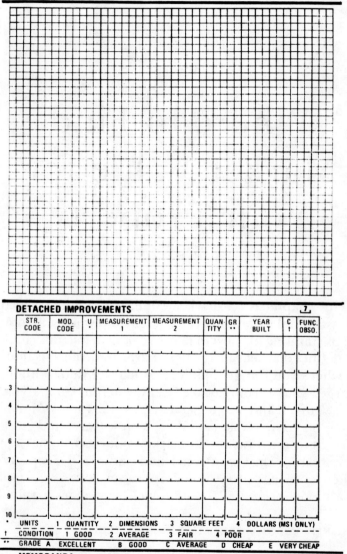

DETACHED IMPROVEMENTS

	STR. CODE	MOD. CODE	U *	MEASUREMENT 1	MEASUREMENT 2	QUAN. TITY	GR **	YEAR BUILT	C †	FUNC. OBSO.
1										
2										
3										
4										
5										
6										
7										
8										
9										
10										

*   UNITS   1 QUANTITY   2 DIMENSIONS   3 SQUARE FEET   4 DOLLARS (MS1 ONLY)

†   CONDITION   1 GOOD   2 AVERAGE   3 FAIR   4 POOR

**   GRADE   A EXCELLENT   B GOOD   C AVERAGE   D CHEAP   E VERY CHEAP

MEMORANDA

CHAPTER 6

Where to Find Market Value for Your Property

This chapter is on market value, that amount which assessors find so hard to keep current and which inflation keeps spiraling upward in many regions. First, this chapter defines market value. Then there are various sections on where you can get opinions of market value without charge, what a "comparable" is, how to find comparable sales yourself and how to get market value for your home from this comparable sales data. You will also find guidance here on how to get market value on homes, on vacant land, on commercial and industrial property. When to hire a professional appraiser follows, as well as a model appraisal report for current market value.

DEFINITIONS OF CURRENT MARKET VALUE

Before we define market value, we have to know its important place in the assessment system. The market value of your property is what your real estate taxes are based on; they are based not on your earnings, as with income taxes. In most states though, properties are usually assessed at percentages ranging from ½% to 50% of market value. Yet, all assessment must start with an opinion of current market values of the property. This has to be done before the assessor can multiply his market value opinion by his legal or average assessment rate. Many assessors use state or private cost manuals to classify and grade each property. They then multiply the square feet of the building's habitable area and the road frontage or square feet of the land by manual cost factors to get their total opinion of value.

If the assessor is valuing commercial or industrial or multiple residential properties, he usually uses an Income Approach method to capitalize the net income of the property in order to arrive at his opinion of value. There are sophisticated assessment systems in a few states which use computers to compare actual sales of similar properties to get market value by the Market Approach. Regardless of which method, whether by the more dependable and accurate Market Approach or by the most frequently used and rarely dependable Cost Approach, the assessor starts with an opinion of market value for your property. And so do you when you appeal to reduce your taxes.

Since before recorded history, men have bartered their possessions, exchanging what each owned after agreeing on what each wanted. Now we transfer money for property and we call the medium of this exchange its value in money. Sophisticated definitions involving market value have been developed, mainly based on value meanings our laws and history have given us. For example, "*Market value is the present worth of rights to future benefits arising from the ownership of the property*," according to precedent court decisions. Value continues to be made and exchanged constantly in our society by the free interaction of many factors influencing the desires and needs of buyers and sellers of property. Thus, another definition of market value is, "*Market value is that amount which a property will bring in the open market from a ready, willing and able buyer and willing seller, neither acting under duress nor constraint.*" Such "arms-length" transactions in our free enterprise system establish values as of a particular date. These values are based on such constantly changing factors as property location, type of building improvements, amenities, zoning, available financing, highest and best use, topography, access, utilities, function and condition of the property. Value is also mainly based on what other people are paying for similar properties similarly situated in similar "arms-length" dealings.

WHERE TO GET MARKET VALUE WITHOUT CHARGE

There are various sources for market value. You are not a professional appraiser of real estate. Yet, you have one very important advantage. You own the property and know its neighbors. Besides drawing on your day-to-day knowledge of real estate happenings in your area—who sold, who moved in, etc.—there are various other leads to follow to secure current market value. Many states, such as New York, accept evidence from the following sources on assessment appeals to substantiate market value:

Source 1—Purchase price, if you bought it recently.

Source 2—Construction Cost, plus land value, if you built it recently.

*Source 3—*Comparable sales of similar properties sold recently.

Source 4—Income Approach can be used to capitalize net income of your commercial, industrial or multiple residential property if similar comparable sales are not available. This approach secures market value by multiplying the property's net income by a capitalization factor typical to valuing such properties. In appeal of assessments, the factor rate used by the assessor on such properties can be used in the appeal. (See also Definitions, Appendix III for Income Approach.)

Source 5—Offering prices of similar properties which are for sale can be listed and submitted in the appeal, particularly to demonstrate an upper limit of market value. It can certainly be argued that no one will pay *more* than such offering prices.

What a "Comparable" Is

The Market Approach or Market Data Approach is the best way to get market value. This method compares and adjusts what people are paying for similar properties, or "comparables," in order to estimate the value of the property being appraised. The secret ingredient of this approach to current market value, however, is to get *good* comparables. A good comparable sale must be as close to the subject property geographically, in price, in date of sale, in similar improvements and amenities as your diligent research can reveal. Match apples to apples. Avoid using two-story oranges for one-story ranch apples. For example, if your residential property is a 25-year "colonial" two-story, don't use contemporary design two-year-old one-story ranches for comparables. Most assessors do their valuations by getting lost and out-dated in their Cost Approach arithmetic. Your object in assessment appeals is to counter these improper valuations with a good current opinion of market value. This is accomplished by using good comparables without having to make extensive judgment adjustments because the comparables are not truly comparable. (See later section on how to get market value from comparables.)

How to Find Comparable Sales Yourself

Since you own your property and know your neighborhood, you often know which similar properties were sold recently. You can use this very important local knowledge in your appeal by following up these leads and getting full sales descriptive data from the following sources:

Comparable Source 1—The owners themselves of these similar properties.

Comparable Source 2—Real estate brokers who operate actively in your area can help on your leads and often give you other recent similar sales.

Comparable Source 3—Bank mortgage officers in your bank may help you from their records on your leads as well as other recent similar sales.

Comparable Source 4—The assessor's property cards on your leads will give sales and descriptive data. His deed transfer records book will also give recent sales. If you go through his cards on your neighborhood you will also find other recent sales of similar properties.

How to Get Market Value from Comparable Sales Data

You don't have to have a host of comparables to prove the current market value of your property. More than five is too much; fewer than three is not enough. The important thing is to choose and know these comparables almost as well as you know your own property. Then, if you have selected comparables similar in location and description to yours, there will be less adjustments to make. For example, if all of your comparables are in your same residential subdivision and from the same model, you may only have to make dollar adjustments for changes and condition. In general, if you have good comparables which are similar to your property, your job of getting market value is simple. The procedure is as follows:

Step 1—*List features of your property.* Write down under a column heading the important features of your property, its location, lot size, building description, extras, etc.

Step 2—*List features of comparables.* Under a minimum of three columns alongside your own property column, write down the features of the comparables.

Step 3—*Adjust in dollars for differences.* In a companion column, write down plus or minus dollar amounts for differences between the features of your property and each comparable. Total these plus or minus differences for each comparable to get an "adjusted" value for each comparable when compared to your property. (See Section 18 of the Model VA Appraisal Report at the end of this chapter for an illustration of this adjusting procedure.)

Step 4—*Determine market value for your property.* From the above, based on full consideration, determine what your property's current market value is, not by averaging the adjusted comparable values but by using good judgment. For instance, this full comparable study often leads you to pick one of the comparables as a "Best Comparable." You may determine your own market value as being close to this most similar recent sale with the other comparables buttressing your judgment.

Note particularly Section 18, Market Data, of the VA Appraisal Report form which is at the end of this chapter. This Section 18 is a good example of this Market Approach procedure of listing and adjusting comparables to subject property to secure market value.

How to Get Market Value on Homes, Vacant Land, Commercial and Industrial Property

Market value can be secured on the below listed classes of properties in the various ways shown:

Homes—Use the Market Approach technique primarily and the various other sources when appropriate, such as purchase price, construction and/or cost, offering prices as detailed in prior sections.

Vacant land—Same sources and techniques as homes.

Commercial properties—Use Income Approach by capitalizing net income if there are no other similar property sales. For example, assume net income of a retail store building is $10,000 (from the commercial real estate alone, rents, etc., not from any business conducted thereon.) Then this $10,000 is multiplied by, say, a capitalization rate of 11 to get a value of $110,000 for the property. The rate can be the same as the assessor's capitalization rate or can be built up by analyzing market data of recently sold similar commercial properties, their selling prices and their net incomes. There are also other more complicated ways appraisers use to derive capitalization rates. For assessment appeals done by property owners, it is most expedient to use the same rate the assessor used. If the commercial/industrial property is large or if you disagree with the assessor's capitalization rate, a professional appraiser should be hired. (See following section.)

Industrial Properties—Same techniques as commercial.

WHEN TO HIRE A PROFESSIONAL APPRAISER

There are various circumstances in which it pays to hire a professional appraiser. In most assessment appeals on the average residential or smaller commercial or industrial property, the owner can do the assessment appeal himself. However when the property is large and valuable or when extensive commercial or industrial real estate is involved, it is important that a professional appraiser be hired to give his opinion in writing on market value.

If the appraiser is hired to also represent the owner at an appeal hearing, there are additional fees for his time. Most of the time, an owner can pay for an appraisal report and then submit the report as part of his appeal data, representing himself at the appeal hearings. The vast majority of assessment appeals can be researched and submitted by the owner himself without any paid professional reports.

A MODEL APPRAISAL REPORT FOR CURRENT MARKET VALUE

The following VA completed model appraisal report is a good example of an appraisal report for current market value. Note particularly Section 18 on Market Data.

Form Approved
OMB No. 76-R023I

VETERANS ADMINISTRATION
RESIDENTIAL APPRAISAL REPORT

CASE NUMBER: 000000

1. MAJOR STRUCTURES

	A. TYPICAL COND.	B. BUILT-UP	C. AGE TYPE BLDG.	D. OWN OCCUP.	E. VACANCY	F. ZONING	G. LAND USE CHGS.
NEIGHBORHOOD	FRAME	80 %	3-10	90 %	0 %	RES	STABLE
BLOCK	FRAME	100 %	3-10	95 %	0 %	RES	STABLE

2. PROPER-TY IS: ☒ OCCU-PIED ☐ VACANT
3. BLDG. WARRANTY IN FORCE? ☐ YES ☒ NO ☐ UNKNOWN

4. STATUS OF PROPERTY
☐ A. PROPOSED ☐ B. PREVIOUSLY OCCUPIED (EXISTING, NOT) ☐ C. PREVIOUSLY OCCUPIED ☐ D. IMPROVEMENTS, OR REPAIRS (ALTERATIONS,)

5. CONSTRUCTION COMPLETED BEFORE DATE HEREOF
☐ A. WITHIN 12 CALENDAR MOS. ☐ B. MORE THAN 12 CALENDAR MOS

E. REFINANCING - VETERAN AP-PLICANT OWNS AND OCCUPIES RESIDENCE AS HOME

6. NAME AND ADDRESS OF FIRM OR PERSON MAKING REQUEST (Complete mailing address, Include ZIP Code)

RELIANT SAVINGS & LOAN
1 BANK ST
YOURTOWN, USA

7. PROPERTY ADDRESS (Include ZIP Code)

200 EVEN ST.
YOURTOWN U.S.A.
(ORANGE COUNTY)

8. TYPE OF PROPERTY
☒ HOME
☐ MOBILE HOME LOT

9. MANDATORY HOME ASSOCIA-TION MEMBER-SHIP? ☐ YES ☒ NO

10A. NO. BLDGS. 1
10B. NO. LIVING UNITS 1

11. LOT DIMENSIONS 100 X 100

12. DESCRIPTION

	WOOD SIDING	CINDER BLOCK	SPLIT LEVEL	% BASEMENT	8 NO. ROOMS	DINING ROOM	I KITCHEN	CEN. AIR COND.
DETACHED ☒	WOOD SHINGLE	STONE	BI-LEV	SLAB	3 BEDROOMS	FAMILY RM.		TYPE HEAT. & FUEL GAS H/W
SEMI-DET.	ALUM. SIDING	BRICK & BLOCK	CRAWL SPACE		2 BATHS	UTILITY RM.		ROOFING DESCRIP. ASP SH
ROW ☒	ASB. SHINGLE	STUCCO	YRS. EST. AGE	3	1/2 BATHS	FIREPLACE	X	SEPTIC TANK ASP SH
CONDOMINIUM ☒	BRICK VENEER (FRAME)	BI-LEV STORIES			LIVING RM. L			

2 CAR GARAGE ☒ GAS
CAR CARPORT UNDERGRD. WIRE
WATER (Public) X SEWER (Public) X
WATER (Comm.) SEWER (Comm.)
WATER (Ind.) SEPTIC TANK

13. LEGAL DESCRIPTION

BLOCK 1 LOT 12 OF
MAP OF TALL PINES, FILED
COUNTY CLERKS OFFICE ORANGE
COUNTY 1/10/7—

14. TITLE LIMITATIONS, INCLUDING EASEMENTS, RESTRIC-TIONS, ENCROACHMENTS, HOMEOWNERS ASSOCIATION AND SPECIAL ASSESSMENTS, ETC.

NONE KNOWN

15. OFFSITE IMPROVEMENTS

A. STREET SURFACE:
B. STREET ACCESS ☒ PUB. ☐ PRIV.
C. STREET MAINT. ☐ PUB. ☐ PRIV.

D. ADD'L. IMPROVEMENTS
☐ STORM SEWER
☐ SIDEWALK
☒ CURB/GUTTER

16. REPAIRS NECESSARY TO MAKE PROPERTY CONFORM TO APPLIC. MPR'S

$ _____

17. REMARKS (Complete A through F. Use supplemental sheet or reverse, if necessary.)

A. DETRIMENTAL INFLUENCES — NONE NULL AIRPORTS
B. REAL ESTATE MARKET IN COMMUNITY — SLOW- MANY FOR SALE SIGNS
C. HIGHEST AND BEST USE — RES- PRESENT USE
D. FEDERAL FLOOD HAZARD MAP ISSUED? ☒ YES ☐ NO
E. PROP. IN SPECIAL FLOOD HAZARD AREA? ☐ YES ☒ NO
  If "Yes," complete item
F. EXPLAIN DEPRECIATION — 3 YRS.
PHYSICAL-NOMINAL — ECONOMIC-SEE ITEM 17C

TOTAL ESTIMATED COST OF REPAIRS $ _____

18. MARKET DATA

ITEM	SUBJECT PROPERTY	COMPARABLE NO. 1		COMPARABLE NO. 2		COMPARABLE NO. 3	
ADDRESS		514 Dix Way Yourtown		95 Sycamore Dr Yourtown		50 Elm Pl Yourtown	
SALE PRICE		$ 37900		$ 37000		$ 38500	
TYPE OF FINANCING		Conventional		V.A.		MGIC	
	DESCRIPTION	DESCRIPTION	ADJ.	DESCRIPTION	ADJ.	DESCRIPTION	ADJ.
DATE OF SALE		Sept, 197-	$ 0	Dec, 197-	$ 0	Dec, 197-	$ 0
LOCATION	Res - Good	Equal	0	Equal	0	Equal	0
SITE IMPROVEMENT	Fair to Good	Good	+500	Equal	0	Equal	0
AGE/CONDITION	3 Yrs Fair to Good	2 Yrs Good	+500	12 Yrs Fair to Good	-500	2 Yrs Fair to Good	-500
GARAGE/CARPORT	2 Car Built In	1 Car B.I.	-300	1 Car B.I.	-300	1 Car B.I.	-300
CONSTRUCTION	Frame (Bi Lev)	Frame (Bi Lev)	0	Frame (Split)	0	Frame (Bi Lev)	0
PORCHES, POOL, ETC.	10'x18' Wood Deck	Equal Deck	0	Electric Heat	-2000	Equal Deck	0
ROOM COUNT/SIZE	ROOMS 8 BDRMS 3 BATH 2½ S.F. AREA 1236	ROOMS 8 BDRMS 4 BATH 1½ S.F. AREA 1160	-800	ROOMS 9 BDRMS 5 BATH 2½ S.F. AREA 1350	+3000	ROOMS 8 BDRMS 4 BATH 1½ S.F. AREA 1160	-900
NET ADJUSTMENT (Show (+) or (-) adjustment)		$ -100		$ +200		$ -1200	
INDICATED VALUE OF SUBJECT PROPERTY		$ 37800		$ 37200		$ 37200	

19. PROPERTY SHOWS EVIDENCE OF (Check)

☐ TERMITE ☐ DRY ROT ☐ DAMP-NESS ☐ SETTLE-MENT ☒ NO EVIDENCE

23. DATA	DESCRIPTION	CONDITION
ROOF	A/S	G
FOUND.	Masonry	G
BSMT.	Bi Lev	G
FLOORS	Oak	G
INT. WALLS	Drywall	G
BATH FINISH	Ceramic	G
GUTTERS	Alum	G

26. ANNUAL TAXES

GENERAL $1000 SPECIAL $ OTHER $

27. DOES PROPERTY CONFORM TO APPLICABLE MINIMUM PROPERTY REQUIREMENTS?
☒ YES ☐ NO (If "No" explain on reverse)

24. EQUIP.
☒ NO VALUE
8 Yrs — Ref 6E
Range 10 Yrs

20. ESTATE (Check) ☒ A. FEE SIMPLE ☐ B. LEASE-HOLD

25. OTHER IMPROVEMENTS
S/S + 1 Door
2 Car B.I. Garage
Drive & Walks
Fin. Rec. Room Bath
4 Utility Rm. Overhead
Landscaping (Good)

DESCRIPTION	DEPR. VALUE
No Value	
No Value	
	$4000
	100

21. REMAINING ECONOMIC LIFE (Years) MAIN 40 OTHER

22. COST APPROACH

MAIN 1236	☐ CU ☒ X ☐ SQ	OTHER	RATE PER FT.	$ 25	
			REPLMT. COST	$ 30900	
			PHYSICAL DEP.	$ 1000	
			FUNCTIONAL	$ 300	
			ECONOMIC	$ 6000	
			TOTAL DEP.	$ 7000	
			DEPR. COST	$ 23900	
			TOTAL DEPR. COST OF IMPR.	$ 23900	
			OTHER IMPR. AND EQUIP.	$ 5750	
			LAND VALUE	$ 8500	
			TOTAL DEPR. COST OF PROP.	$ 39150	

28. ESTIMATE FAIR MONTHLY RENT TIMES RENT MULTIPLIER (if applicable)
$ 340 × 110 = $ 37400

TOTAL $ 0

29. RECONCILIATION

A. MARKET APPROACH	B. COST APPROACH	C. INCOME APPROACH (if applicable)
$ 37200	$ 37350	$ 37400

TOTAL $ 37350

30. I ESTIMATE "REASONABLE VALUE" $

31. ESTIMATED REASONABLE VALUE $ 37200

☒ "AS IS" ☐ "AS REPAIRED" ☒ "AS COMPLETED"

NOTE: No determination of reasonable value may be made unless a completed appraisal report is received (38 U.S.C. 1810). I HEREBY CERTIFY that (a) I have carefully viewed the property described in this report, INSIDE AND OUTSIDE, so far as it has been completed; that (b) it is the same property that is identified by description in my appraisal assignment; that (c) I HAVE NOT RECEIVED, HAVE NOT AGREEMENT TO RECEIVE, NOR WILL I ACCEPT FROM ANY PARTY ANY GRATUITY ANY GRATUITY OR EMOLUMENT OTHER THAN MY APPRAISAL FEE FOR MAKING THIS APPRAISAL; that (d) I have no interest, present or prospective, in the applicant, seller, property, or mortgage; that (e) in arriving at the estimated reasonable value I have not been influenced in any manner whatsoever by the race, color, religion, national origin, or sex of any person residing in the property or in the neighborhood wherein it is located. I understand that violation of this certification can result in removal from the fee appraiser's roster.

32. SIGNATURE OF APPRAISER Samuel T. Conrad

33. DATE SIGNED 4/6/7

CHAPTER 7

When to File Timely Appeals

Prior chapters covered assessment history, procedures, errors, research and market value. This chapter stresses timely assessment appeals. The most carefully researched appeal based on well-documented market value can expose multiple glaring assessors' errors. Yet, the appeal will be thrown out, at least for the current taxing year, if the appeal does not come in before the correct legal deadline. First, this chapter shows you who can file an appeal for assessment/tax reduction. Then there is a section on how to apply informally to the assessor for reduction. If unsuccessful in such informal appeal there is guidance here on how to go to the next formal stage if unsatisfied with the assessor's determination. Finally, two special sections analyze why the assessment appeal process has mainly been used by large investors and property owners, and also how you can join with taxpayer and public interest groups for joint appeal action.

Who Can File an Appeal

If you own the property, you are always the one who can put in an appeal. However, there are other kinds of interest in property besides ownership which give appeal rights in many taxing districts. For instance, in New York State, any one of the following persons "aggrieved" by an assessment may file a complaint by completing the state's written complaint form under oath:

1. The *owner* of the property.
2. The *purchaser* of the property who is under contract to buy it.
3. The *tenant* of the property who is required by his lease or agreement to pay the property taxes.
4. The *attorney* for the owner, purchaser or tenant.
5. Anyone who *represents* the owner, purchaser or tenant.

Many of the thousands of taxing districts have similar but varying requirements. In some districts, appeals can even be filed on the property of others by a neighbor or other person who claims that underassessment is involved. In every appeal, it is most important that you first secure and check out current state and local appeal regulations.

How to Apply Informally to the Assessor for Reduction

As an affected "aggrieved" property owner, tenant, purchaser or representative, you start with the following step-by-step procedure in informal assessment appeals to the assessor.

Step 1—Go to the assessor's office and request to see all the public assessment records on your property.

These usually include a standard description and valuation card, filed by tax map and section, block and lot number, as well as by address.

Step 2—Review your assessment card thoroughly for errors in description.

Step 3—Review all computations for errors.

Step 4—Review records of similar properties. Concentrate particularly on those properties in your immediate area or block to see whether your assessment is fair and equal to these similar properties in that similar location.

Step 5—Check whether your assessment is illegal or should be exempt. Request and review information from the assessor or state office to determine whether all or part of your property should be free from or exempt from taxes because of location, your age, your income, your veteran status, farm, forest land, mineral or other legal tax relief or exemption. (See Appendix I.)

Perhaps such a preliminary review and its results will convince the assessor to reduce your assessment without your proceeding to the next formal appeal stage. This often occurs. I've represented property owners as an appraiser. These property owners have often taken my review to their assessors who subsequently made substantial assessment reductions.

Oregon is one of the few states in this country with progressive, statewide, comparatively up-to-date assessment practices, mainly computerized. It also is the only state which really makes an effort to inform its citizens about the various ways they can appeal. It even tries to make the pills of property taxes less bitter by putting its appeal instructions in cartoon form. The following excerpted cartoon boxes of this Oregon Department of Revenue pamphlet, "Appeal!!" are particularly appropriate to this initial, informal appeal stage.

How to Determine Filing Date

Appendix I gives you in table form information on where and when to appeal if informal review with your local assessor is not successful. A quick glance through this 50-state table should convince you that—like everything else in assessment work—nothing is ever uniform, particularly appeal filing dates. Some give definite and indefinite dates, such as "10 days prior to 1st June Monday," or, "before 25 days from assessment notice." Others give "depending" dates like, "before 15 days from assessor's decision on appeal."

Regardless of how varied, and sometimes how "tricky," the date may read in your taxing district, it is your responsibility to find out and appeal on time. Otherwise, the least you lose is a whole year. You may even lose your chance for a reduction. By the time the next "grievance" period comes around, there may be a whole new set of changed circumstances and all your research and evidence may be out of date and no longer pertinent. Some states give out very little information in assessment notices on tax bills regarding your assessment or time period within which you can appeal. Use Appendix I in this book as a starter and check with your local assessor always for any local differences. Remember! Complaints must be filed by the *last* day of the grievance period.

How to Go to the Next Stage If Unsatisfied

Appendix I lists by state the various county and state Boards of Tax Appeals or Boards of Equalization which

receive assessment appeals. In a few localities, assessors themselves even judge appeals on their own assessments. Different states have different procedures. As with filing dates, many of the states and sometimes even many of the taxing districts in the same state have different ways of handling your formal appeal. The burden of proof still rests on you to get that proof in on time, to the right district or state person or agency.

In general, the following procedure to ensure formal, timely, complete appeals filed with the proper agency will apply practically everywhere. (In all cases, check with your assessor for local differences.)

Step 1—Get proper appeal forms. Well ahead of deadlines, get all the appeal and instruction forms from your local assessor or from your state assessment office.

Step 2—Review and complete the complaint form. (See Chapter 9, completed model complaint form with attached evidence.)

Step 3—Submit this formal appeal form. This can usually be submitted to the assessor or mailed to the proper appeal board or brought to the appeal board if permitted by local regulations.

Step 4—Attend formal appeal hearing. See also Chapter 9 on how to argue your appeal.

Step 5—Submit for higher review. If appeal is denied, whether by assessor, if he is the first formal appeal judge, or by an appeal board, be certain to apply for appeal review by the next higher appeal authority if provided for in regulations.

Step 6—Go to court if all else fails. If all administrative appeals have failed, determine whether to go on to a court suit. In most cases, particularly where large and valuable properties are involved, an attorney

and appraiser should be hired for this stage. However, I have done appraisals for homeowners who
have gone on to argue and win court tax reductions
themselves, usually by settlement before trial. (See
Chapter 10.)

WHY REAL ESTATE INVESTORS ARE THE MAIN USERS OF THE APPEAL PROCESS NOW

Most appeals are still made by investor-owners of large
and valuable properties, and most tax reductions are
granted to such investors.

Yet most inequities and most overassessments in this
unfair old system are on properties such as homes and
other smaller real estate parcels owned by the average
American property owner.

The owner-investor of the large industrial building
or office skyscraper or shopping center turns the tax
reduction case over to his lawyers to make the appeal.
The small homeowners or farmers or small businessmen
property owners have not been using the appeal process
in any significant numbers. This is mainly because the
system is not designed in most areas to make it easy to
understand how it works and how to appeal.

The large investor can just pay for the professionals
to figure out his appeal and he gets the reductions in
return for his fees. The small owner generally has to do
it himself. The rewards are there. In my own hometown,
33 percent of all the homeowners who appealed in one
year received tax reductions up to $4300 and tax savings
up to $175 per property *per year*! The trouble is only 18
applicants appealed out of 15,000. Yet, it is generally
conceded that in most assessment taxing districts at least
one-third of the assessments are wrong.

All it takes to lower your taxes is the desire not to be overassessed and over-taxed, the will to do something about it, as the big investors do, and the appeal guidance in these pages.

WHEN TO JOIN WITH TAXPAYER AND PUBLIC INTEREST GROUPS

Most appeals can be successfully waged alone, for one's own property. However, there are situations when joint action may help get tax reductions for you and your neighbors. Assessment is mostly a political system. Assessors are mainly elected rather than appointed. They are sensitive to group action by voter-owners, particularly if there are grounds for the group complaint. The following are possible types of appeal situations which may merit your getting together with your neighbors to appeal.

1. If a particular neighborhood appears to be over-assessed compared to others.
2. If the homeowners in a particular recently built housing development appear to be regularly over-assessed as newcomers.

If the group does decide to appeal, much more leg-work on collecting assessment-sales ratio evidence and market data comparables can be done because there are more people to do the research.

The statistics are impressive. Most people don't make assessment appeals. Of those who do, the majority of individual appeals are granted. Group appeals usually are even more successful since research on matters such as assessment-sales ratios can be more conclusive and appeals can be professionally paid for and presented.

However, whether individual or group, the odds of winning an assessment/tax reduction appeal are in your favor. This is mainly because of the antiquated, unequal nature of the assessment system itself. It just takes patience to understand and make order out of this disorderly system and use its built-in inequities to win your assessment/tax reduction.

CHAPTER 8

How to Make Sure You're Assessed Fairly and Equally

A key element of appeal research and of very effective appeal evidence is the matter of unequal and unfair assessments. Prior chapters have given general information on why this is so prevalent in assessing. This chapter is where you learn to do the actual detailed assessment review to determine whether your property is fairly and uniformly assessed compared to similar properties. You'll also note here that merely because your assessment is practically always well below current market value, this does not mean your assessment is correct. Follow-up sections give guidance on how to check if your assessment is fair compared to your neighbors' and how to check whether your property should be partially or totally exempt from taxes. There is also a detailed work-plan section which gives three separate worksheets—one for checking your assessment rate, one for showing assessors and appeal boards that your property is assessed *more* than similar ones even though they're *equal* to yours, and one detailed worksheet to determine and show that your property is assessed the *same* as others even though they are worth *more*.

ASSESSMENT LESS THAN MARKET VALUE DOES NOT MEAN YOUR ASSESSMENT IS CORRECT

Often, assessors and appeal boards will ask you during interviews and hearings, "Would you sell your property for what it's assessed?"

This question is only a strategic one to keep you confused about this confusing assessment system. In practically all cases, assessments are lower than market value for a variety of reasons. Some states, by law, require that different classes of property be assessed at different percentages usually ranging from ½% to 50% of market value. Other states require 100% of market value assessment, but this just doesn't work out in practice because the system can't do the job of keeping values and assessments up-to-date. A variety of other reasons including errors, ineptitude and sometimes favoritism also cause similar properties to have unequal assessments and better properties to have similar or lower assessments than inferior properties.

So, you can answer this question about selling by saying, "No," without harm to your appeal. In fact, this question-answer reveals the central fault of the whole assessment system—its lack of uniformity—as it pertains to the real estate taxes you pay. You can turn this type of cross-examination to your own appeal advantage by showing through research in the assessor's own records that he is assessing your property unfairly compared to other properties. The whole point is, neither you nor anyone in the taxing district would sell for less than market value because practically all assessments are at less than 100% value. By this same token, a full answer to this question could be, "No, I would not sell at the assessment figure. But neither would my neighbors with similar properties who you've assessed lower than me. And here are pictures and data on twenty properties I've researched to show how unfair my assessment is!"

Most Properties Not Assessed Uniformly at Same Percentage of Market Value

For all the reasons listed in the prior section, most properties are not assessed uniformly. Even if the original appraisal of the property by the assessor is correct and current, then the assessment percentage,

$$(Assessment \div Market\ Value = Percentage)$$

is usually wrong. Appendix I lists many states which have laws requiring assessors to assess at varying percentages of market value. Other states have no such requirements, but the assessments are almost invariably at less than 100%, usually far less. Even in those few areas where courts or states require full valuation, assessments are rarely at 100%. So you can always count on lower than market value assessments practically everywhere. You can't count on uniformity.

Similarly even if there is an out-of-date low appraisal on your property, it does not mean that you're fairly assessed or under-assessed. Say your house is worth $60,000 today, appraised on the assessor's card for $40,000 and assessed at $30,000 or 75% of assessor's appraisal.

Everything's fine, right? Wrong! You first have to find out whether 75% is the rate at which properties in your area are being assessed. There are three ways to get this rate:

First, ask the assessor. Whatever rate he gives you will probably be incorrect and certainly rarely uniform.
Second, do the research yourself as shown in later paragraphs.
Third, check with your state assessment office. Some states compute and make available these assessment-sales ratios for all their taxing districts. Contact your state office for this rate but be cautious in its use; state rates usually are an *average* of *all* classes of properties in the district, whether residential, commercial or industrial, etc., and may not be specific enough to your type of property for proper appeal evidence.

The best way is the *second* method mentioned above. Do the research yourself. Get from a real estate broker or even from the assessor's own records, selling prices on about 20 to 25 same class of properties in your area during the last year. Divide the assessment of each by the selling price to get each assessment-sales rate. Then add up all the rates and divide by the total number of properties to get the average assessment-sales ratio. Compare this to what the assessor told you the assessment rate is on your property. If there is a substantial difference, this is good evidence for an appeal. (See assessment-sales ratio worksheet later in this chapter.)

This inherent defect in the system—its apparent inability to treat taxpayers uniformly—becomes your appeal leverage. Check it out. Take the time to see if you're fairly assessed at the legal or proper assessment percentage and at the same percentage of market value as the similar properties of your neighbors. Do the detail work shown in the later work-plan section of this chapter to gather good evidence for your appeal. Remember: If you and your neighbor own houses worth $40,000 each but yours is assessed at $20,000 and his at $15,000, with a local tax rate of $70 per $1000, you would pay $1440 and he $1050.

How to Check If Your Property Should Be Totally or Partially Exempt from Taxes

As taxes mount, more and more types of properties owned by persons and institutions become partially or totally exempt from taxes.

Appendix I lists some of the more recent "relief" exemptions many states now give their hard-pressed taxpayers.

The following checklist of all types of legal exemptions is offered here as a general checklist for you to check whether any may apply to you or your property. You should always check this out finally in your own district for exact requirements if you believe you qualify.

CHECKLIST OF PROPERTY TAX EXEMPTIONS AND RELIEF

_____ Veterans
_____ Disabled veterans
_____ Paraplegic veterans
_____ Widows of veterans
_____ Schools
_____ Religious purposes
_____ Hospitals
_____ Charitable purposes

_____ Agricultural purposes
_____ Industrial exemptions
_____ Hardship cases
_____ Property tax credits against state income taxes (includes renters)

____ Public purposes

____ Historic sites

____ Certain non-profit purposes

____ Cemeteries

____ Senior citizens

____ Private property used for community purposes

____ People with low income

____ "Homestead" exemptions

____ Scientific purposes

____ Blind people

____ Public airports

____ Certain housing authorities

____ Mining purposes

____ Indian lands

____ Gold-star parents

____ Fallout shelters

____ Reforestration purposes

____ "Circuit-breaker" relief, based on income

____ Nursing-homes, non-profit

____ Urban renewal properties

____ "Abatement" exemptions for certain types of new and rehab construction

WORKSHEETS TO HELP YOU GATHER APPEAL DATA

Various worksheets are in this section. You will find the data you need for your assessment appeal at the assessor's office on his public assessment record cards, at real estate brokers, at your friendly mortgage officer banker. Regardless of source, the way to gather evidence for successful appeals is by systematic research and documentation. Worksheets help you do this research and help convince the appeal boards later.

This first worksheet is for developing an area or local assessment-sales ratio to check on whether you are assessed at the legal or average rate of assessment uniformly:

ASSESSMENT-SALES RATIO WORKSHEET

STEP 1—ESTABLISH ASSESSMENT RATE FOR YOUR PROPERTY.

(a) Use the following formula:

Assessed Value ÷ Full Value = Rate of Assessment

or

(b) Assessed Value × 100 ÷ Rate of Assessment (for your area) = the amount the assessor maintains is the full value of your property.

thus

_____ ÷ _____ = _____

_____ × (100 ÷ _____) = _____

STEP 2—COMPARE YOUR ASSESSMENT RATE TO AVERAGE RATE OF ASSESSMENT FOR OTHER PROPERTIES. Get about 20 to 25 actual recent sales in the area, divide this total into the total of their assessments to find the assessment-sales rate. Thus:

	Assessment ÷	*Sales Price* =	*Assessment Rate*
1.	$35,000	$60,000	58%
2.	$45,000	$70,000	64%
3.	$55,000	$80,000	70%
4.	$40,000	$65,000	62%
5.	$50,000	etc.	etc.
6.	etc.	etc.	etc.
20.	etc.	etc.	etc.
25.	etc.	etc.	etc.

TOTAL __% ÷25 =
AVERAGE ASSESSMENT RATE

The following two worksheets involve simpler yet often equally effective appeal methods. Instead of finding about 25 actual sales to prove actual assessment-sales ratio, all you do here is compare your property's assessment to assessments of others. Both worksheets are for residential properties although they can be adapted for other types.

First, there is a worksheet to help you compare your property to about a dozen or so *similar* properties in your area which have *lower* assessments.

Second, there is a companion worksheet to help you review and compare your property to another dozen or so of *better* properties in your area which have *equal* assessments.

In both types of these assessment reviews, you get all the information you need from the assessor's public records. You have to review his cards on each property for descriptive and assessment information to compare them to your own property. In both worksheets, the entries on the first line pertain to your own property. Each of the following entries on the "comparables" should have major differences stressed under "Remarks." *Take a picture of each assessment comparable.*

WORKSHEET

FOR COMPARISON OF SIMILAR PROPERTIES

WHICH HAVE LOWER ASSESSMENTS

	TAX MAP SECT.	BL.	LOT	OWNER	SQ. FT.	TYPE & STORIES	AGE	RMS	BRs	BTHS	SIZE LOT	ASSESSED	REMARKS
1.												$	(Your Property)
2.													(comparables)
3.													"
4.													
5.													
6.													
7.													
8.													
9.													
10.													
11.													
12.													
13.													

Miscellaneous Notes (Use numbers as references.)

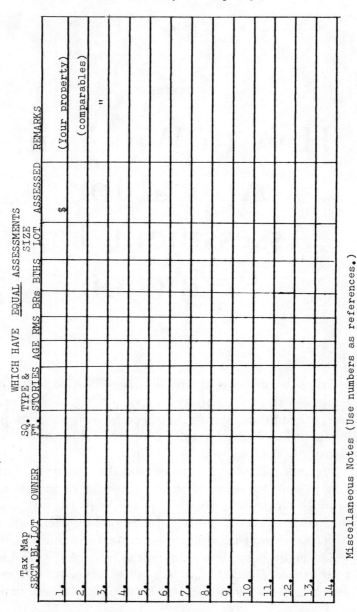

CHAPTER 9

How to Win Your Appeal for Assessment/Tax Reduction

The sole purpose of this entire book is to help you reduce your property taxes. Our ancient assessment/taxing system has become even more hopeless as it has had to handle property values in our increasingly complex modern society.

Preceding chapters have recited the origins and history of this system so that you can understand how it came to its present hopeless state. As in chess or war, the battle is better won if the opponent—the system which takes your tax dollars—is known and understood.

Succeeding chapters detailed the many ways in which your assessment can be wrong. They stressed that these assessment errors can be used to help reduce your taxes.

They also gave you methods for locating these errors, for finding market value for your property, for ensuring timely appeals and for making certain you're assessed equally with your neighbors.

So this chapter is the one where all this background and all these appraisal and assessment review methods come together for the sole purpose of helping win your appeal for assessment/tax reduction. The first section puts it all together so that a well-documented appeal can be made. There is also a detailed assessment appeal work-plan checklist. An excellent graphic cartoon series then illustrates how Oregon taxpayers are helped through this assessment appeal process. Finally, there is an actual model appeal complaint form with attached evidence including an excerpted appraisal report.

HOW TO PUT IT ALL TOGETHER AND SUBMIT A WELL DOCUMENTED APPEAL

Your assessment can be most unjust, unequal, unfair, overassessed or illegal. Yet, the burden of proof is on you. Unlike our system of law, our assessment system considers you "guilty" until you prove yourself "innocent." Therefore, complete review and documentation of evidence is the name of this appeal game. Class assessment appeal actions and joint assessment appeals by neighbors are sometimes successful, but even when you join others, you still have to know and make appeals yourself.

ASSESSMENT APPEAL
WORK-PLAN

STEP 1—RESEARCH
   (A) *Determine current value* of your property from the following sources: (See Chapter 6 also)

_____ *Purchase price* if you bought the property recently.

_____ *Construction Cost*, plus land value or cost if you built it recently.

_____ *Comparable Sales* of similar properties, similarly located, recently sold.

_____ *Income Approach* of commercial, industrial and other properties.

_____ *Offering Prices* of similar properties which are for sale (as an indication of upper limit of value).

_____ *Written Appraisal Report* by a professional appraiser.

(B) *Determine if you are overassessed* by taking the following basic review steps: (See also Chapters 3, 4, 5, and 8 and Appendix I)

_____ *Total assessment of your property* should be checked first at the assessor's office. This is best done when the assessment roll for the current year is publicized, although it can be done on a preliminary basis anytime prior. In any event, don't wait until you receive your tax bill. It's too late then for that tax year.

_____ *Check for errors* in description or arithmetic on the assessor's property record card.

_____ *Check whether legal.* Do you qualify for partial or whole exemptions? Is the property in the taxing district, etc., etc.? (See prior chapters.)

_____ *Check whether assessment is higher than market value.* This is not often the case with residences but can usually be found in other types of property. For example, larger vacant land tracts in depressed sections of the northeast are often overassessed compared to their market value, because of low demand for such types of property.

—— *Check if assessment is based on too high an appraisal.* Sometimes assessor's records or your tax bill show this information on value and assessment rate. Ask the assessor what he has valued your property at and what the tax rate is, if the records or your tax bill do not contain this information.

—— *Check if you have been assessed at uniform assessment rate* (see Chapter 8). Remember! Even if your assessment is far lower than market value, the assessment rate is often wrong and not uniform and can cause overassessment.

—— *Check if your assessment is higher than similar properties* in your neighborhood (see Chapter 8 for guidance and worksheets). Check if your property assessment should be lower than others because it has less amenities or is more run down or has inferior location. (See Chapter 4 for Construction and Site Influence Checklist.)

STEP 2—PRESENT INFORMAL COMPLAINT TO ASSESSOR In most states, assessors are authorized to make corrections and reductions in assessments, particularly if you have found errors in description of your property or in computation. If you're turned down in this informal review with the assessor and your research has convinced you that you are over-assessed and over-taxed for any of the above reasons, then go on to the next formal appeal step in this checklist.

STEP 3—PREPARE AND FILE FORMAL APPEAL COMPLAINT

—— *Secure all the proper complaint forms and instructions.*

_____ *Check for proper filing date or period* (see Appendix I).

_____ *Fill out the complaint form* (see later section in this chapter).

_____ *Attach all the evidence* you have gathered in your research, the worksheets you have used, the appraisal report you have secured or the market investigation you have done, the photos you have taken, etc. Whatever has convinced you or the appraiser you hired that your property deserves an assessment reduction should be part of your formal appeal complaint.

_____ *File the complaint* either with the assessor for submission to the formal grievance board or file it with the board directly. In some states, the complaint form can be brought to the board when you appear during its public hearings. In other states, the complaint form has to be submitted before the hearing. In all cases, be guided by the local instructions for filing assessment complaints.

STEP 4—APPEAR AT THE HEARING. You should always attend personally or send your representative. The best documented written appeal can go for nought if you're not there to discuss it with the board members who are local members of the community. There shouldn't be an inference that your case wasn't important enough for you to come before the local board personally or send a representative.

_____ *Be respectful* to these neighbor board members. No matter how you may have been "dumped on" in overassessment, don't let anger ruin your case.

_____ *Do help your facts speak.* In your presentation, emphasize the important, the central basis of your appeal. Answer all questions to the best of your

ability. You are in a good position. You own and
know your property best. You're familiar with
your neighborhood.

_____ *Don't lecture!* Don't claim inability to pay the taxes.
You're there to show the property is overassessed
and over-taxed, not that you find it increasingly
difficult to pay these taxes. It may be true and
they may be sympathetic to your plight but they
can't do anything about it legally. They can only
consider your appeal regarding your assessment.

_____ *Know your rights.* Prepare yourself for the hearing
by reviewing this book and by carefully going
over your local assessment appeal instructions.
Some complaint forms and some board members
may even try to frighten you by saying they have
the power to increase as well as decrease on appeal. This has hardly ever happened. Or a mem-
ber may ask if you would sell your property for
the amount of the assessment. Chapter 8 gives
you the reply.

*STEP 5—IF DENIED, GO ON TO THE NEXT APPEAL
LEVEL.* In certain states, denial by one grievance board
means automatic review by a higher board (see Appendix I). In other states, you have to voluntarily re-file the
appeal (the same complaint with the same appeal evidence) to the higher board, within the proper filing time.

STEP 6—DECIDE WHETHER TO GO TO COURT, if all
else fails. See Chapter 10 for guidance on when and how
to go to court.

Mr. "Tuned-out" Taxpayer Learns How to Appeal
in Oregon

In Chapter 7, some cartoon boxes were excerpted
from an excellent Oregon cartoon pamphlet called

"Appeal!" Oregon is no doubt the most progressive state in its attempts to enlighten its citizens and modernize its assessment procedures. The following additional cartoon boxes from this pamphlet continue Mr. "Tunedout's" journey through Oregon appeal procedures. They also graphically portray many of the appeal steps we have shown.

A COMPLETED MODEL COMPLAINT FORM WITH ATTACHED EVIDENCE

The following New York State Assessment Complaint form has been completed as a model from an actual appeal appraisal done by the author. In this case, the property owner only had to show that the assessment was higher than current market value. There was no need to gather evidence of partial assessment at a lower than market value percentage since the assessment far exceeded value by appraisal and assessments were supposed to be at full market value in this area. This property was located in a depressed county in the Northeast where reduced market demand had plummeted land tract values after an initial boom. Identification, photos and certain data and exhibits on buildings have been omitted and the appraisal report condensed. This is a good example of a successful appeal. Original land assessment was reduced from $122,500 to $89,500 and taxes from $4316 to $3153, each year! (A yearly savings of $1163!)

Purpose of Appraisal—This appraisal is made for the purpose of arriving at an opinion of the Fair Market Value of the subject property if offered for sale on the open market under conditions prevailing Sept. 22, 19— and is based on a physical inspection of the parcel, analysis

COMPLAINT ON REAL PROPERTY ASSESSMENT FOR 19 —

BEFORE THE BOARD OF ASSESSMENT REVIEW FOR <u>Town of ——</u>

(County, City, Town or Village)

(Read general information and instructions, form EA-38-a)

PART ONE: GENERAL INFORMATION

1. Name of owner or owners of property.   Post Office Address

   —— Associates Corp.   c/o James ——
                                Box ——
                                ——, N.Y

2. Name and address of agent or representative of owner, if agent or representative is filing application.

3. Description of property or tax map number as it appears on the Assessment Roll.

   Section 2 Block ——   Lot ——

4. Location of property (street, road, highway number, and city, town or village).

   About 475' Southeast of Route —— (by Deeded R.o.w) T/o ——, N.Y

5. Type of property:

   ☐ Residence   ☐ Farm   ☐ Resort   ☐ Apartment   ☐ Industrial

   ☐ Business (indicate type) _____

   ☐ Vacant Land   ☒ Other (specify) 64.4 Acres and Barn

6. Assessed valuation appearing on the Assessment Roll.

   Land $ 122 500   Total $ 122500

PART TWO: GROUNDS FOR COMPLAINT ON ASSESSMENT

A. ☐ **INEQUALITY**

The assessment is erroneous by reason of inequality: the property is assessed at a higher percentage of full (market) value than the average of all other property on the assessment roll.

Full (market) value of property: $_____

Percentage of full value at which complainant believes his property should be assessed is _____ % , based on one or more of the following:

1. ☐ The latest equalization rate for the city, town or village in which the property is located (enter latest equalization rate: _____ %).

2. ☐ A sample of other parcels on which complainant relies for objection (list parcels on a separate sheet and attach).

3. ☐ Statements of the assessor or other local official that property has been placed on the roll at _____ %.

Complainant believes the assessment should be reduced to $ _____

B. ☒ **OVERVALUATION**

The assessment is erroneous by reason of overvaluation: the assessment exceeds the full (market) value of the porperty

Full (market) value of property: $ _45100_ Assessed valuation of property: $ _122,500_

Amount of overvaluation claimed: $ _77400_

Complainant believes the assessment should be reduced to $ _45100_

C. ☐ **INCORRECT PARTIAL EXEMPTION**

Complainant believes he is entitled to a partial exemption granted for _____ (specify veteran's, aged, clergy, etc.).

If application for exemption was filed, attach copy of application to this complaint. If you do not have a copy, you should request the assessor to submit it to the board of assessment review.

Amount of exemption claimed: $ _____ Amount granted, if any: $ _____

1. ☐ Refusal to grant all or part of claimed exemption results in an erroneous assessment by reason of inequality. (If you check this box, fill in item A. above).

2. ☐ Refusal to grant all or part of claimed exemption results in an erroneous assessment by reason of overvaluation. (If you check this box, fill in item B. above).

D. ☐ **ILLEGALITY**

The assessment is illegal for the following reason:

1. ☐ Property is totally exempt.

2. ☐ Property is totally outside the boundaries of the city, town or village.

3. ☐ Property cannot be identified from description or tax map number on the assessment roll.

4. ☐ Other (explain)

PART THREE: INFORMATION TO SUPPORT COMPLAINT

. The full (market) value on taxable status date for this year was $ 45100

. Information to support the full (market) value claimed:

1. ☐ Purchase price of property $ _____

   a. Date of purchase _____ _____

   b. Terms: ☐ Cash ☐ Contract ☐ Other (explain)

   c. Amount of mortgage, if any $ _____ Year mortgaged _____ Rate of interest _____ %

   d. Relationship between seller and purchaser

   e. Personal property, if any, included in purchase price (furniture, livestock, etc.)

2. ☐ If property is insured, state amount: $ _____

3. ☐ If property has been recently offered for sale:

   When and for how long: _____

   How offered: _____

   Asking price: $ _____

4. ☒ If property has been recently appraised:

   When: SEPT 22, 14—, UPDATED 5/8/- By whom: SAMUEL T. BARASH, REAL ESTATE APPRAISER

   Purpose of appraisal: CURRENT MARKET VALUE

   Appraised value: $ 45100

5. ☒ Describe any buildings or improvements located on the property and present condition:
   OBSOLETE FULLY DEPRECIATED BARN- NO VALUE

   Year of Construction: _____

6. ☐ If buildings have been recently remodeled or constructed, state:

   Year remodeled or constructed _____ Date commenced: _____ Date completed: _____

   Cost: $ _____

   Complainant is prepared to submit construction cost details where available. Such information may be attached and submitted with complaint, if desired.

7. ☐ If property is leased or rented, complainant is prepared to submit rent schedules and other pertinent information. Such information may be attached and submitted with complaint, if desired.

   ☐ If property is income producing, commercial or industrial property, the complainant is prepared to present detailed information about the property, including rental income, operating expenses, sales volume and income statements. Such information may be attached and submitted with the complaint, if desired.

   ☐ If property is specialized property (i.e. utility property) complainant is prepared to submit detailed facts concerning the property. Such information may be attached and submitted with the complaint, if desired.

   ☐ Explain briefly any additional facts relied on. (Use attachments, if necessary)

PART FOUR: VERIFICATION

City
Town   of ———— , N Y   ss:
Village

County of ————

———— ASSOCIATES CORP , being duly sworn, says that he is
                                              (owner)
the OWNER ———— (agent of the owner) of the real property described
above; that the statements contained in this complaint are true to the best of his knowledge;
that he claims to be aggrieved by the assessment; and that he hereby makes application to the
Board of Assessment Review to have same reviewed and revised as indicated in this complaint.

Sworn to before me this ————

day of AUGUST 19 ——   SIGNATURE
                                              JOHN ————
                                            Signature of owner or agent
                                            ———— ASSOCIATES CORP

———— SIGNATURE + SEAL
Commissioner of Deeds or Notary Public
(or other officer authorized by law
to administer oaths)

SPACE BELOW FOR BOARD OF ASSESSMENT REVIEW

☐ Assessment erroneous by reason of inequality.

   Assessed valuation on tentative roll: $ ———— Assessment Claimed: $ ————

                 Assessment determined by Board: $ ————
☐ Assessment erroneous by reason of overvaluation:

   Assessed valuation on tentative roll: $ ———— Assessment claimed: $ ————

                 Assessment determined by Board: $ ————
☐ Assessment illegal.

   Grounds:

   Disposition:
☐ No Change in Assessment

4

of sales of comparable properties and consideration of all factors which affect value including amenities, depreciating influences, zoning, utility, location, topography, present and potential uses.

Location—The property, 64.4 acres of land, lies in the County of _____, N.Y., along the town line separating the Town of _____ from _____ in the Town of _____, about 475′ southeast of NYS Route __ via an easement R.O.W. across adjoining lands on the northeast. Access to the site is good because it is about 2 miles west of NYS Route __ and the Interchange of the New York State Thruway with NYS Route __, approximately __ miles from New York City. (See location maps.)

Ownership—_____ Associates Inc., P.O. Box __, _____, N.Y.

Fair Market Value—As used herein, the term market value is defined as that price which a ready, willing and able buyer would pay an equally qualified seller in an arm's-length transaction, neither buyer nor seller under compulsion and both knowledgable regarding the transaction.

Environs and Economic Milieu—Present usages in the vicinity are primarily scattered rural residential and a large egg farm east of the property which occasionally has been know to produce odors depending upon season, winds and atmospheric conditions. In this vicinity and in _____ county in general, there had been much land speculation and some development in the past decade. However, in 19__, coincident with the energy shortage, recession and other larger economic factors, commuter demand from economically ailing New York City disappeared in this region. As mortgage money for development tightened and NYC policemen, firemen and other civil servants lost or feared the loss of their jobs, they gave up home seeking here and acreage sales for development and speculation practically ceased. As the Valuation section of this report will review later, a total of only 7 large acreage arm's-length sales occurred in Orange County since November of 19__, none exceeding $1000 per acre. Against this backdrop of quiescent sales market for land sales for residential development, this parcel's comparatively good location counts for little in this outer metropolitan rim suburb which does not have a good local employment base. In appraiser's opinion, this area and neighborhood will not change its limited scattered residential lot nature for many years, if at all.

Topography (See attached Geodetic Map)—The parcel is fairly regular, measuring 615' × 2063' × 1015' × 1663' × 450' (see attached property sketch), has no road frontage, only a deeded R.O.W. and has about 10 acres of good level land on the northwest end of the property where the improvements—an obsolete, no value barn and some outbuildings—barely stand. As the land falls away to the southeast behind the buildings, the gradients steepen to a ravine, studded with a pond and wet areas, then climb steeply up a heavily forested grade—approximately 25%—to a ridge at the southeast end of the parcel. (See photo montage.) Since the highest and best use of the land by its zoning and location is for residential development, these steep grades on approximately 75% of the building would seriously limit the number of lots and buildings and seriously increase the cost of road and site improvements.

Zoning—Town of _____ zoning law specifies RAM zoning for the northwesterly 925' end of the property; the southeasterly 1138' is zoned R-1-A. Hence, we have RAM on 17.5 acres approximately, requiring minimum 1-acre lots for 1-family houses, 80% larger lots for 2-family houses; camps, hotels, poultry houses, riding academies, airfields, kennels, fur farms, hospitals, cemeteries, gravel pits are also permitted. R-1-A zoning is on approximately 26.5 acres, permitting 1-family on minimum 1-acre; religious buildings, parks, schools, agriculture and golf courses.

Highest and Best Use—Based on its topography, location and zoning, this parcel's highest and best use is for future one-family residential on large-lot subdivided lots, dictated by zoning and topography.

Easements and Encumbrances—This property has deeded R.O.W. over existing driveways on the "premises adjoining on the west to the public road, Route __."

Legal—Town of _____ Tax Map Section __, Block __, Lot __. Deed Liber __, Pg. __, 7/25__ on file __ County Clerk Office.

Assessment—$122,500 for 64.4 acres of land.

Taxes—$_____

Method of Appraisal—The Comparable Sales or Market Approach to value has been used to appraise the land. All large acreage sales occurring in _____ County since November __ have been studied. The appraiser has also considered in his review the fact that there are reported to be hundreds of large acreage parcels unsold in the last two annual _____ county tax sales, further depressing buyer interest and sales. Appraised in fee simple.

Valuation (COMPARABLE SALES APPROACH)—

Comparable	Sold	Description	Comment
1. —— to —— Ave. —— NY Tax Map —— Liber ——/——	$65000 10/9/— $1000 per acre.	Rolling, good developable land zoned Resid. and Agric. *65 acres*, vacant.	Location not as good as subject, much better topography, considerable road frontage. Subject considered 30% inferior.
2. —— to —— —— —— Rd., T/O —— Map — Liber —	$63500 7/27/— $600 per acre	Rolling, good land, zoned Res. & Agric., *106* acres, vacant	Larger parcel. Similar comment as No. 1. Subject considered 15% superior.
3. —— to —— —— Rd., ——, NY	$115000 9/2/— $700 Ac.	Rolling, good land, Res. & Ag. 159 Ac. vacant	Larger, sim. nearby, considerable road frontage, level, considered equal.
4. —— to —— —— Rd., ——, NY	$125000 1/— $800	Steep grades, Res. & Ag., 159 Ac., vac.	Similar nearby loc. topo., good road frontage, 12% inferior

DATED: September 22, ——   SAMUEL T. BARASH
                                  REAL ESTATE APPRAISER

CHAPTER 10

If All Else Fails When to Go to Court

This final chapter is for that minority of assessment appeals which are turned down by review boards. The first section covers the important question of when to hire a lawyer. There is guidance on how to testify in court, including some illustrative excerpted minutes of court testimony by the author in an assessment appeal court case. Timely court appeals are also particularly stressed here. Finally, to avoid such untimeliness denials, there is an all-state timely court appeals "countdown" chart.

WHEN TO HIRE A LAWYER

If the assessment review board rejects your appeal, you have to decide whether to go to court and appeal the decision. You have to compare the legal expenses you will incur to the amount of taxes you can save if you win the appeal. Most of the time, only owners of large land tracts, multiple dwellings or large commercial-industrial properties can meet this legal cost-tax savings yardstick. It is most important also that the property owner or his representative make certain that any court appeal is filed by the required legal filing date. (See later sections in this chapter on timely court appeals and on all-state "countdown" chart.)

There have been successful assessment appeals in court by laymen representing themselves in court. One of my appraisal clients even took my affidavit of appraisal letter to court himself and won his suit by settlement with the county attorney before trial. Assessment reduction—$72,000 to $55,000; net tax savings each year—$500 + ; total out-of-pocket cost—$50; (appraisal letter) legal notice of protest court filing fee—$5.

How to Testify in Court

If you appear in your own case, lay persons can testify only as to facts, not opinions. If you are accepted as an expert witness possessing particular knowledge or experience not common to laymen, then you may be permitted to give your expert opinion. General guidance on how to testify includes the following:

1. Be respectful to all court officers including the attorney who cross-examines you. Dress conservatively.
2. Avoid reflex answers; think first, then speak. (The court minutes do not denote pauses.)
3. Try not to fidget. Be unhurried.
4. Don't try to be witty.
5. Don't "act" with voice or gestures and inflections.
6. Laughter is out of place. Smile when appropriate.

7. Speak carefully, clearly. Avoid repetitive habits like, "You know. . . ."
8. Answer questions concisely. Don't run on.
9. Don't lose your temper. Don't raise your voice.
10. If you don't know, say so.
11. The manner in which you state your qualifications and present your evidence is important. Be modest, sound capable but not boastful.

Of course, always be guided by your attorney who handles your court appeal.

SOME ILLUSTRATIVE TAX COURT TESTIMONY

Recently, the author appraised an 84-acre, old, non-working farm for the landowner at $550 per acre, plus buildings. The subsequent court decision reduced the assessment from *$134,800* (84 acres @ $1500 per acre plus $13,000 in buildings). Net tax savings dollars each year—$2200 +. The following excerpted minutes of the author's testimony in this case illustrate some of the guidance given in this chapter. Note particularly testimony on use, comparables and value.

Q. What factors did you consider in your comparability analysis?
A. I had to find similar property, suffering from similar difficulties, in terms of terrain, access, rock, grades. One of the problems in establishing value is dealing with the highest and best use of a tract of land. In this case, the highest and best use of this land in today's market is for residential development. Now, the problem inherent in this land, either barring or limiting residential development, made me seek comparables which bore similar characteristics relating to such highest and best

use. And I did find certain comparables which, in my opinion, were similar by such criteria and were similarly situated.

Q. Tell us your comparables, as set forth in your Appraisal Report, Exhibit 4.

A. I have a comparable, Schoenman to Spell, date of sale, February, 197___, identified by Liber ___, Page ___, in the amount of 89.127 acres, located on the Chester Tax Map, Section ___, Block ___, Lot ___. Selling price, $53,500, vacant land. In my remarks contained in my Appraisal report which affected my judgment on the adjusting of this particular comparable to the subject property, this property, Schoenman to Spells, not only was unimproved but had a better access road, Gibson _____ Rd. to the property, which itself has a right-of-way frontage only. It has similar steep lands, but no flooding meadows. When I viewed the comparable during my own personal inspection, I did not see rock in the areas I went to, although I did see steep grades. I saw boulders.

Q. What value did you put on it?

A. I don't put value on a comparable. I did the computation, the arithmetic. If you divide $53,500.00 by 89, you get a rate of $600.00, plus or minus, which is just a factor we feed into our appraisal process and subsequently come up with an opinion, not a computation.

Q. What is your second comparable?

A. The adjoining piece of ground assembled by the same purchaser, Spells from _____, purchased also in February, 19___, Liber ___, Page ___, 20.439 acres, Chester Tax Map, Section ___, Block ___, Lot ___; price, $12,500.00. The computation rate would be $600.00, plus or minus, per acre. And the same comments on this as in my Schoenman comparable. It's abutting land with the same contours, the same grades and the same access road. My third comparable is George G. Roesch Estate to _____, October, 19__, located at the corner of _____ Road and _____ _____ Road, Chester Tax Map Section __, Block __, Lot __, Liber __, Page __. And talking about 78 plus or minus acres for $74,000.00, the acre rate would be computed at $950.00, plus or minus. It's vacant land, with a much better access road than the subject has; similar road frontage to subject; it has no flooding meadows and it is not as rocky, but it is steep. And, of course, the subject property, to answer your original question, after analyzing these comparables, not computing this rate, but my best judgment, I appraised the acre rate at $550.00 per acre for the Davidson farm.

Q. Plus the 8.7 acres?

A. The $550.00 per acre applies to the 84.26549 net total acreage for the Davidson farm, which includes the 8.7 acres at the same rate.

Q. You placed the total value of the two parcels mentioned herein as $76,500.00?

A. That's right.

Q. Can you explain that figure?

A. We multiply out—my computation net total figure is 84.26549 acres. I multiplied that by $550.00, and it gave me a total of $42,132.00. Then I added to that $22,100.00 for the house and barn, which gave me $68,446.00. Then I deducted $1,100.00, to represent the same acre rate that the house stood on one acre. The barn also stood on one acre. I took $1,100.00 off, and came up with $67,346.00, which I rounded off to $67,500.00. You must understand the premise. The premise is, in my opinion, the house is worth no more than $21,000.00, no matter what factors go into it. And in my opinion, the barn is worth no more than $1,100.00;

the house and barn will stand on an acre. If so, I had to remove the $550.00 from my calculations.

Q. Based on your experience and background in the real estate field, what do you consider the best use for the land?

A. The highest and best use for any land in this section of the town of Blooming Grove would be for residential development. As I stated in my report here and I will quote: "The access, topography and subsoil limitations completely bar the property's highest and best use development for residential purposes and severely limit its zone use for horse farm value. It has no value for dairy farming, both intrinsically and within the economic current milieu.

Q. Tell us what it can be used for.

A. Recreational—

Mr. Thomas: Objection. He is beyond the scope of his appraisal. If he is going to say the highest and best use is recreational, it should have been in here.

The Referee: I think the purpose of the whole thing is to show the value of the land. He is stating what cannot be used. I think it is a proper question, what is the best use. Answer the question.

A. Its present use is its best future use, to be used in a limited recreational way.

The Importance of Timely Court Appeals

If the original assessment appeal is partially or totally denied by lower level assessment authorities (see Appendix I), then appeal to the courts can be taken in most states. Timely court appeal is critical at this stage because if you miss the legal court date, you have to start all over again next year . . . from the beginning, with original review boards etc. Conditions can change and your evidence will probably be obsolete.

Also, if you win, you lose the benefits of retroactivity of reduction to the date of original appeal. The All-State Timely Appeal "Countdown" Chart which follows has been excerpted from International Association of Assessing Officials data and is furnished for information purposes only. You or your attorney should check your local area for any changes in current dates or procedures. The dates in the chart pertain to appealing period after prior lower review decision.

AN ALL-STATE
TIMELY COURT APPEALS "COUNTDOWN"

STATE	COURT	DATES IF AVAILABLE
Alabama	Supreme Court	Within 30 days
Alaska	Superior Court	—
Arizona	Superior Court	On or before Nov. 1
Arkansas	County Court	On or before 2nd Monday in Oct.
California	(Only certain board decisions can be court appealed; dates vary)	
Colorado	(Only public utilities may appeal to courts by Aug. 1st of following year)	
Connecticut	County Court Common Pleas	Within 2 months
Delaware	County Superior Court	Within 30 days
(Wash.) D.C.	Superior Court (Tax Div.)	Within 6 months after Oct. 1st
Florida	Circuit Court of County	—
Georgia	Court of Appeals or Supreme Court	—

STATE	COURT	DATES IF AVAILABLE
Hawaii	(1) Tax Appeals Court (2) Supreme Court	(1) On or before Apr. 9th (2) Within 30 days of tax appeals court decision.
Idaho	District Court	Within 30 days
Illinois	(Local board decisions are final; some cases may be taken to courts.)	
Indiana	Various courts	Within 30 days
Iowa	County District Court	Within 20 days
Kansas	(State equalization board decisions are final; some cases may go to courts.)	
Kentucky	Circuit and Appellate Courts	—
Louisiana	District Court	By Nov. 1st
Maine	County Superior Court	—
Maryland	(1) State Tax Court (2) Court of Special Appeals	(1) — (2) —
Massachusetts	Supreme Judicial Court	—
Michigan	Court of Appeals	Within 20 days
Minnesota	(1) Tax Court (2) Supreme Court	(1) — (2) —
Mississippi	(1) County Circuit Court (2) Supreme Court	(1) Within 10 days (2) Within 6 months
Missouri	(1) County Courts or Circuit Courts (2) Supreme Court	(1) Within 30 days (2) —
Montana	Court of Competent Jurisdiction	Within 30 days

STATE	COURT	DATES IF AVAILABLE
Nebraska	District Court or Supreme Court	Within 10 days
Nevada	Court of Competent Jurisdiction	—
New Hampshire	County Superior Court	Within 6 months
New Jersey	Supreme Court Appellate Div.	—
New Mexico	Court of Appeals or County District Court	Within 45 days
New York	Supreme Court in assessment judicial district	Within 30 days of assessment roll
North Carolina	(For court review, claimant has to sue to get back tax.)	
North Dakota	District Courts	—
Ohio	(1) County Court of Common Pleas (2) Higher Court of jurisdiction	(1) Within 30 days (2) —
Oklahoma	(1) District Court (2) Supreme Court	(1) Within 10 days (2) —
Oregon	(1) Tax Court (Small claims) (2) Supreme Court	(1) Within 30 days (or 6 months to 2 years in certain cases) (2) —
Pennsylvania	(1) County Court Common Pleas (2) Superior Court (3) Supreme Court	(1) — (2) Within 90 days (3) Within 45 days
Rhode Island	County Superior Court or Superior Court (in certain cases)	Within 3 months of payment due date

STATE	COURT	DATES IF AVAILABLE
South Dakota	Circuit Court	Within 30 days
South Carolina	(May go to court only after exhausting all administration procedures)	
Tennessee	(Board actions final but subject to judicial review.)	
Texas	District Court	—
Utah	Supreme Court	—
Vermont	(1) County Court (2) Higher Court	(1) Within 20 days (2) —
Virginia	(1) County or City Court (2) Higher Courts	(1) Within 2 years of Dec. 1st (of affected tax year) (2) —
Washington	(Taxpayer may sue in court to recover taxes.)	
West Virginia	(1) County Court (2) Circuit Court (3) Supreme Court (if assessment over $50,000)	(1) Before Feb. 28th (2) Within 30 days (3) —
Wisconsin	Circuit Court	Within 90 days
Wyoming	District Court	Within 60 days

Appendix I

WHERE AND WHEN TO APPEAL AND OTHER ASSESSMENT TAX DATA

If informal review with your local assessor is not successful, the following 50-state table lists where and when to file your property tax appeal. If these formal agency appeals are denied, your final recourse is to go to court (see Chapter 10). There is also information here, state by state as available, on admissible appeal grounds on assessment-sales ratios, on partial/full value, on the comparatively recent exemption concepts of "homestead" and "circuit-breaker" tax relief (see Appendix III—Definitions), on assessor qualifications and whether local assessors work from state assessment manuals. These procedures have been compiled from direct contact with state officials and from the International Association of Assessing Officers and generally cover most appeal situations. However, some cities and counties may have varying requirements, and legislative changes do occur. It is advisable to check directly with each local assessor or state agency in individual cases. See Appendix II for a list of State Assessment Officials.

ALABAMA

WHEN TO APPEAL—10 days prior to 1st Monday in June

WHERE—County Board of Equalization

ADMISSIBLE GROUNDS FOR APPEAL—If higher than similar property; if higher than legal standards; assessment-sales ratio not admissible

PARTIAL/FULL VALUE—Residential—15%; commercial—25%; public utilities—30%

TAX RELIEF—Homestead—$2000 assessed value; over 65 (income limit)—$5000 market value

ASSESSOR QUALIFICATIONS—6-year terms; no experience necessary

STATE MANUAL—Yes

ALASKA

WHEN TO APPEAL—Before 30 days from assessment notice

WHERE—Board of Equalization, city or borough

ADMISSIBLE GROUNDS—If higher than similar nearby property; assessment-sales ratio admissible

PARTIAL/FULL VALUE—Full Value

ARIZONA

WHEN TO APPEAL—Before 15 days from assessor's decision on appeal

WHERE—Board of Equalization (county); Board of Tax Appeals (state)

ADMISSIBLE GROUNDS—If higher than legal standard; if higher than similar nearby property; assessment-sales ratio admissible; appeal may be based on *classification* of property (see following paragraph)

PARTIAL/FULL VALUE—Mines and RR—60%; utilities—50%; commercial—27%; rented or leased residential properties (apts., duplexes, etc.)—21%; agricultural and vacant lands—18%; homes assessed at full value (recent assessment-sales ratio—15%)

TAX RELIEF—None

ASSESSORS—4-year terms; no experience/education necessary

STATE MANUAL—Yes

ARKANSAS

WHEN TO APPEAL—Between 1st and 3rd Monday in August

WHERE—Equalization Board (county)

ADMISSIBLE GROUNDS—If higher than legal standards; assessment-sales ratio admissible

PARTIAL/FULL VALUE—All classes—20%, audited by state—3% sample appraisal of all classes of property (recent ratio 19.57% based on 1956 cost manual)

TAX RELIEF—State refund on property tax for citizens over 65 and unable to pay

ASSESSORS—2-year term; no experience/education necessary

MANUAL—Yes (outdated—1956)

CALIFORNIA

WHEN TO APPEAL—July and August

WHERE—Assessment Appeals Board (county) or Board of Equalization

ADMISSIBLE GROUNDS—If higher than similar nearby property; if higher than legal average for district; assessment-sales ratio admissible

PARTIAL/FULL VALUE—Homes—25%; certain

classes of open space land, non-profit golf courses and certain municipally owned properties assessed at differing partial rates

TAX RELIEF—Homeowners exemption of $7000 full cash value on owner-occupied homes, senior citizen assistance, veterans and welfare exemptions. (The so-called "Jarvis Initiative" passed by referendum vote in 1978 limiting property taxes to 1% of market value, as shown on 1975–76 tax bill or thereafter, the appraised value of real property when purchased, built or sold after the 1975 assessment. Maximum increase each year thereafter for inflation—2%)

ASSESSORS—4-year term; no experience/education necessary

STATE MANUAL—Yes (for public utilities only)

COLORADO

WHEN TO APPEAL—Before 2nd Wednesday in July

WHERE—Board of Equalization (county); Board of Assessment Appeals (state)

ADMISSIBLE GROUNDS—If higher than legal standards; assessment-sales ratios not admissible

PARTIAL/FULL—*Homes*—30% based on the following factors as they apply: location, function, depreciated replacement cost, market value based on comparison and trade and income approach; *agricultural*—land value based on earnings capitalized at 11½%; *all other property*—30%; equipment, livestock, merchandise, supplies, mines, oil and gas, solar heating and cooling—percentage varies from 50% to 100%

TAX RELIEF—Senior citizen, disabled real property, renters and mobile home owner receive tax credits or refunds

ASSESSORS—No experience/education necessary

MANUAL—State Cost Manual to estimate replacement cost; State Goods Manual to estimate inventory value

REMARKS—Agency can reduce or increase assessments to correct errors made by assessor and to equalize values within county

CONNECTICUT

WHEN TO APPEAL—February

WHERE—Board of Tax Review (city)

ADMISSIBLE GROUNDS—If higher than nearby similar property; assessment-sales ratio admissible

PARTIAL/FULL VALUE—70% all properties

TAX RELIEF—65 and over

ASSESSORS—Terms and experience requirements vary by towns

MANUAL—No

DELAWARE

WHEN TO APPEAL—Varies by county

WHERE—Varies by county

ADMISSIBLE GROUNDS—*New Castle County*—Must show that market value for subject property is less than estimate made by assessor; *Sussex County*—Market value used to determine cost schedules, appeal must show property is not assessed in accordance with market for base year; *Ken County*—assessment higher than legal standard and assessment-sales ratio are admissible grounds; may also appeal *classification* of property for valuation purposes

PARTIAL/FULL—Full value in cash

TAX RELIEF—Over 65 "homestead"

ASSESSORS—Appointed; no requirements

FLORIDA

WHEN TO APPEAL—Before July 15th

WHERE—Board of Tax Adjustment (county); Dept. of Revenue (state)

ADMISSIBLE GROUNDS—Higher than legal standards; assessment-sales ratios admissible

PARTIAL/FULL VALUE—100% value basis, except agricultural land at 10%; raw materials at 1%

TAX RELIEF—"Homestead," $5000; aged and disabled exemption, $10,000; "homestead" property tax deferral for low income owners

ASSESSORS—4-year term—no qualifications necessary

MANUAL—Yes

REMARKS—Owner can challenge assessment by auctioning property at stipulated price below assessed value

GEORGIA

WHEN TO APPEAL—Before 10 days from assessment notice

WHERE—Board of Equalization (county)

ADMISSIBLE GROUNDS—Appeal can be based on fair market value, equalization of assessed value or taxability of property; assessment-sales ratio admissible

PARTIAL/FULL VALUE—40% of fair market value based on market, cost and income approaches

TAX RELIEF—Senior citizen "homestead" exemptions in varying amounts depending upon age and income

ASSESSORS—Appointed for 6 years or longer; certain education and experience requirements

MANUAL—No

HAWAII

WHEN TO APPEAL—Before 25 days from assessment notice

WHERE—Board of Review (district) Tax Appeal Court (state)

ADMISSIBLE GROUNDS—If higher than legal standard; if higher than similar nearby property; if higher than average for district; assessment-sales ratio admissible

PARTIAL/FULL VALUE—60%, except for agricultural lands, which are assessed based on agricultural rather than highest and best use

TAX RELIEF—*"Homestead,"* $12,000; includes homes leased for 5 years and leased cooperative apartments and certain other residences under certain conditions

ASSESSORS—Appointed civil servants with civil service standards

STATE MANUAL—Yes

IDAHO

WHEN TO APPEAL—Before 2nd Monday in July and on 4th Monday in November

WHERE—Board of Equalization (county) Board of Tax Appeals (state)

ADMISSIBLE GROUNDS—If higher than similar nearby property; generally appeals are discussed on appraised market value rather than assessed value; assessment-sales ratio admissible if all classes of property not uniform within county

PARTIAL/FULL VALUE—Recent value to sales ratio 14.26% (must be 20% by 1982 according to State Law)

TAX RELIEF—"Circuit-breaker" and "homestead" relief provided according to various state laws

ASSESSORS—Elected 4 years; no qualifications necessary

MANUAL—A State Appraisal Cost Factor Guide is furnished

ILLINOIS

WHEN TO APPEAL—Before 20 days from assessment notice

WHERE—Board of Review or Appeals (county) Property Tax Appeal Board (state)

ADMISSIBLE GROUNDS—If higher than similar nearby property; assessment-sales ratio admissible; Board can apply township equalization multipliers

PARTIAL/FULL VALUE—33⅓% of Market value except in Cook County, where there are different classes of property assessments but overall level must be 33⅓% of Market value. Farm land assessed by separate three-part formula

TAX RELIEF—"Circuit-breaker" and "homestead" relief based on income, age and disability; Appeals Board makes initial decision on exemptions

ASSESSORS—Elected and appointed for 4-year terms; no qualifications necessary for elected; exam and 2-year experience necessary for appointed

INDIANA

WHEN TO APPEAL—Before 30 days from assessment notice

WHERE—Board of Review (county)

ADMISSIBLE GROUNDS—If higher than legal grounds; assessment-sales ratio not admissible

PARTIAL/FULL VALUE—33⅓% of "true cash value"

for all classes as determined by use of State Manual (*not* based on market value)

TAX RELIEF—Over 65—$1000 deducted from tax value

ASSESSORS—Elected for 4 years; no qualifications necessary

MANUAL—Yes

IOWA

WHEN TO APPEAL—Between April 16th and May 5th

WHERE—Board of Review (city or county)

ADMISSIBLE GROUNDS—If higher than legal standards; if higher than similar nearby property; assessment-sales ratio admissible; Board has broad power to equalize assessments, although power not exercised fully

PARTIAL/FULL VALUE—Homes assessed at full market value; assessment-sales ratios are determined for each class of property locally, (no single statewide ratio); agricultural property assessed solely on productivity

TAX RELIEF—"Circuit-breaker" refunds property tax or rent paid for disabled persons, certain surviving spouses, those aged 65 and over with less than $9000 income and for mobile home owners; "homestead" credit of $4500 given to all Iowans who file an *annual* application with local assessor; "homestead" special tax credit to disabled veterans and those with military service tax exemptions

ASSESSORS—Appointed for 6 years; must pass exam and have 2 years' experience

MANUAL—Local assessors are required to use the state manual.

KANSAS

WHEN TO APPEAL—Between April 1st and May 15th

WHERE—Board of Equalization (county) Board of Tax Appeals (state)

ADMISSIBLE GROUNDS—If higher than similar nearby property; assessment-sales ratio admissible

PARTIAL/FULL VALUE—The state constitution requires that all real and personal property be assessed at a uniform and equal rate

TAX RELIEF—State rebates for those aged 60 and over, based on income

ASSESSORS—Appointed and elected

KENTUCKY

WHEN TO APPEAL—Before 5 days after first Monday in June

WHERE—Board of Assessment Appeals (county)

ADMISSIBLE GROUNDS—If higher than legal standards; assessment-sales ratio admissible; board must review comparables provided by assessor

PARTIAL/FULL VALUE—All classes of property assessed on 100% "fair cash value" market basis; latest assessment-sales ratio is in 90–100% range

TAX RELIEF—"Homestead" relief of $6,500 in assessment, subject to cost of living adjustment every 2 years ($8,900 recently)

ASSESSORS—Elected for 4 years; must take exam to go on ballot; once elected, paid and supervised by state

MANUAL—Real Estate Appraisal Manual (outdated) and Property Assessment Administration Manual.

LOUISIANA

WHEN TO APPEAL—Varies

WHERE—Tax Commission (state)

ADMISSIBLE GROUNDS—Taxpayers can contest assessments by appealing to the assessor, to the tax commission, to local (Parish) Boards of Reviewers or to District Courts; *no* specific admissible grounds for appeal

PARTIAL/FULL VALUE—Homes, vacant land and agricultural—10%; other—15%

TAX RELIEF—"Homestead" exemption for all homeowners

MAINE

WHEN TO APPEAL—Before 1 year from assessment

WHERE—Board of Commissioners (county) or Board of Assessment Review (local)

ADMISSIBLE GROUNDS—If higher than legal standards; if higher than average for district; assessment-sales ratio admissible

PARTIAL/FULL VALUE—Partial based on local assessor's judgment; full in unincorporated areas assessed by state; minimum standards of 50% after 1979, all areas

TAX RELIEF—Relief granted per elderly householders Rent and Tax Refund Act

ASSESSORS—Elected and appointed for varying terms —experience requirements in only 6 of 497 municipalities

MANUAL—No

MARYLAND

WHEN TO APPEAL—Before 30 days from assessment notice

WHERE—State Property Tax Assessment Appeal Board, Maryland Tax Court

ADMISSIBLE GROUNDS—If higher than similar

nearby property; assessment-sales ratio admissible; taxpayer may appeal under- or non-assessment of other taxpayer

PARTIAL/FULL VALUE—Full value

TAX RELIEF—Homeowners' and renters' relief based on income; relief for over-65s based on income

ASSESSORS—Appointed by local bodies after exams by state; no qualifications necessary

MASSACHUSETTS

WHEN TO APPEAL—Before October 1st

WHERE—Board of Assessors (town or city); Appellate Tax Board (state) or Commissioner's (county)

ADMISSIBLE GROUNDS—If higher than legal authority; if higher than similar property; if higher than legal average for district; assessment-sales ratio admissible

PARTIAL/FULL VALUE—Full value

TAX RELIEF—Varying exemptions for those over 70

ASSESSORS—Elected and appointed; no qualifications necessary

MICHIGAN

WHEN TO APPEAL—Before first part of March

WHERE—Board of Review (local) Michigan Tax Tribunal

ADMISSIBLE GROUNDS—If higher than legal average for district; assessment-sales ratio admissible

PARTIAL/FULL VALUE—50% of full value, all classes

TAX RELIEF—Substantial property tax credit from income tax to a maximum of $1200 per household; includes recognition of part of rent as property tax and gives extra credit to senior citizens

ASSESSORS—Most are elected, some appointed; terms not fixed except for supervisor-assessors at 2 years; experience requirements set by State Assessors Board
MANUAL—Yes

MINNESOTA

WHEN TO APPEAL—Before 1 year from assessment notice
WHERE—Board of Review (local), (authorized to adjust assessments, must give notice and hearings if increasing); Board of Equalization (county); Board of Equalization (state)
ADMISSIBLE GROUNDS—If higher than similar nearby property; assessment-sales ratio admissible
PARTIAL/FULL VALUE—Homes—40%; homesteads—20% (balance—33⅓%); commercial, industrial and public utility—43%; lakeshore and farm—30%; timberland—20%; agricultural homestead (up to 160 acres)—16% (balance—30%); State Limited Value Law also limits yearly changes in value to 10% of the previous assessment or 25% of difference between actual full market value and prior assessment, whichever is greater
TAX RELIEF—$15,000 base value on each homestead is assessed at lower rates; income adjusted refunds on qualified tax for homesteads; annual credits up to $475 for general homesteads; up to $800 each year on homes for blind or disabled persons
ASSESSORS—Appointed—must be licensed or certified by State Board of Assessors, based on knowledge of taxation; county assessor's term 4 years, local assessor's term indefinite
MANUAL—Yes

MISSISSIPPI

WHEN TO APPEAL—Before first Monday in August

WHERE—Board of Supervisors (county); Tax Commission (state)

ADMISSIBLE GROUNDS—If higher than similar nearby property; assessment-sales ratio not admissible

PARTIAL/FULL VALUE—20% for all classes; state officials attempting to equalize differing assessment percentages which vary considerably from locality to locality

TAX RELIEF—"Homestead" relief of $5000 to all homeowners

ASSESSORS—Elected; no qualifications necessary

MANUAL—Yes

MISSOURI

WHEN TO APPEAL—Before 2nd Monday in July

WHERE—Board of Equalization (county)

ADMISSIBLE GROUNDS—If higher than legal standard; if higher than nearby similar property; assessment-sales ratio admissible

PARTIAL/FULL VALUE—33⅓% of true value, all classes of property

TAX RELIEF—"Circuit-breaker" for homeowners and renters over 65, based on income

ASSESSORS—All elected except 3 appointed assessors in St. Louis, St. Louis County, and Jackson; length of term 4 years

MONTANA

WHEN TO APPEAL—Before third Monday in July

WHERE—Tax Appeal Board (county) State Tax Appeal Board

ADMISSIBLE GROUNDS—If higher than nearby similar property; assessment-sales ratio admissible

PARTIAL/FULL VALUE—All classes assessed at 35% of full cash value

TAX RELIEF—Senior citizens 62 or older, $11,000 or less income; renters, homeowners, mobile homeowners get percentage of property tax as either credit or refund based on sliding scale of income, ranging from 10 to 90% of tax

ASSESSORS—Elected; after election, assessor-appraisers must pass state certification test and take 36 hours of training each year; term is 4 years

MANUAL—Uses Marshall-Swift Residential Manual Service

NEBRASKA

WHEN TO APPEAL—Between April 1st and May 1st

WHERE—Board of Equalization (county); Board of Equalization and Assessment (state) (or District Court)

ADMISSIBLE GROUNDS—If higher than similar nearby property; assessment-sales ratio admissible

PARTIAL/FULL VALUE—35% of market value

TAX RELIEF—Homeowners aged 65 and over, based on income

ASSESSORS—Elected for 4 years; must pass test by tax commissioner

NEVADA

WHEN TO APPEAL—Between December 1st and January 10th

WHERE—Board of Equalization (county); Board of Equalization (state)

ADMISSIBLE GROUNDS—If higher than legal standard; if higher than nearby similar property; assessment-sales ratio admissible; may appeal as not the same as like property

PARTIAL/FULL VALUE—35% of full cash value

TAX RELIEF—"Circuit-breaker" for homeowners and renters aged 62 and over, based on income

ASSESSORS—Elected for 4-year terms, no qualifications necessary

NEW HAMPSHIRE

WHEN TO APPEAL—Before 4 or 6 months from tax bill issuance (fee $15)

WHERE—Board of Taxation (state), 4 months; or Superior Court of County, 6 months

ADMISSIBLE GROUNDS—If higher than legal average for district; assessment-sales ratio admissible; appellant may satisfy through use of comparables

PARTIAL/FULL VALUE—Full value basis; every other year state required equalization show assessment-sales percentages ranging from 10% to 100%

TAX RELIEF—Exemptions for elderly based on income

ASSESSORS—Elected and appointed; no qualifications

MANUAL—Yes

NEW JERSEY

WHEN TO APPEAL—Before August 15th

WHERE—Board of Taxation (county); State Division of Tax Appeals

ADMISSIBLE GROUNDS—If higher than legal standards; if higher than similar nearby property; if higher than legal average for district

PARTIAL/FULL VALUE—Full value; statewide average ratio of assessed value to true value in mid-seventies was 78.06%, ranging from 13.33% to 140.49% equalization; farmland assessed at its value for use rather than at market value

ASSESSORS—Elected and appointed; must be 4-year college graduates or have equivalent appraisal or assessor years of experience and pass a state certification test

NEW MEXICO

WHEN TO APPEAL—Before 30 days from property valuation notice

WHERE—Valuation Protests Board (county); appeals by property owner only

ADMISSIBLE GROUNDS—If higher than legal standards; if higher than similar nearby property; if higher than legal average for district; assessment-sales ratio admissible

PARTIAL/FULL VALUE—Homes—33%; special methods used for agricultural property, livestock, mobile homes, mineral property, airlines, railway, pipeline companies and others

TAX RELIEF—Low income tax credit

ASSESSORS—Elected for 2-year terms; no qualifications necessary

NEW YORK

WHEN TO APPEAL—Before 3rd Tuesday in June

WHERE—Local Board of Assessment Review

ADMISSIBLE GROUNDS—If higher than legal standard; if higher than similar nearby property; if higher than legal average age for district; assessment-sales ratio admissible. The recent extremely important precedent *Guth* court decision allows property owners to *recoup* taxes they have paid in *prior* years if their appeal proves that the assessment of their property was excessive compared to the average assessment of other properties in their categories

TAX RELIEF—No "circuit-breaker" or "homestead" exemptions but some assessment exemption for aged with incomes ranging from $3000 minimum to $7200, depending upon local ordinances

PARTIAL/FULL VALUE—State law and several court decisions, including *Hellerstein v. Assessor, Town of Islip*, state all property shall be assessed at full value and that full value is market value; however, local assessors have still been mainly assessing fractionally. The New York State Constitution establishes the following tax limits: counties—between 1½ and 2% of full value; cities under 125,000—2%; city school districts—between 1¼ and 2%; villages—2%; towns, central school districts and special districts—no limit

MANUAL—No current required state manual; various assessment manuals have been issued

NORTH CAROLINA

WHEN TO APPEAL—Before June 30th

WHERE—Board of Equalization and Review (county)

ADMISSIBLE GROUNDS—If higher than legal standards; if higher than similar nearby property; assessment-sales ratio *not* admissible

PARTIAL/FULL VALUE—All property is assessed at full (market) value except agricultural, which is appraised at use value; all property reappraised every 8 years

TAX RELIEF—"Homestead" system excludes first $7500 in assessed value of real and personal property for residential purposes; 65 and over and disabled

ASSESSORS—Appointed for 2 years; no qualifications necessary; must be certified by state based on courses in appraisal and course in tax law
MANUAL—No

NORTH DAKOTA

WHEN TO APPEAL—Before 2 years from assessment
WHERE—Local taxing District Governing Board; Board of Commissioners (county); Special State Tax Appeals Board
ADMISSIBLE GROUNDS—If higher than nearby similar property; assessment-sales ratio admissible; to increase an assessment, notice to owner must be sent and hearing date set
PARTIAL/FULL VALUE—Assessments on full value basis; recent ratio of assessed value to sales price 13%
TAX RELIEF—Senior citizen tax credit—age 65 and disabled, owner occupied, income maximum $8000; assessed value reduction, inversely to income
ASSESSORS—Elected and appointed; must meet certain educational and experience standards
MANUAL—Yes

OHIO

WHEN TO APPEAL—Before December 20th.
WHERE—Board of Revision (county) Board of Tax Appeals (state)
ADMISSIBLE GROUNDS—If higher than legal average for district; assessment-sales ratio admissible; appellant may complain of overvaluation, underevaluation, discrimination valuation or illegal valuation
PARTIAL/FULL VALUE—50% of full value
TAX RELIEF—"Circuit-breaker" for homeowners 65

and over based on income varying assessed value reductions
ASSESSORS—Elected for 4-year term; no qualifications necessary

OKLAHOMA

WHEN TO APPEAL—Before 10 days from notice of increase
WHERE—Board of Equalization (county)
ADMISSIBLE GROUNDS—If higher than similar nearby property; assessment-sales ratio admissible; complaint is against the amount of assessment, whether caused by amount of appraisal or by level of assessment
PARTIAL/FULL VALUE—Not to exceed 35%; average residential assessment ratio in 1976 was 13.70%; assessed valuations are only 10 to 15% of fair cash value
TAX RELIEF—"Homestead" exemption of the first $1000 of assessed valuation; additional "homestead" exemption of $1000 of assessed valuation for families with gross income of $4000 and less; "circuit-breaker" for those aged 65 and older or disabled whose household income is $6000 and less, may receive up to a $200 property tax refund
ASSESSORS—Elected for 4-year term; no qualifications
MANUAL—No (there is a suggested schedule for personal property)

OREGON

WHEN TO APPEAL—Between first and third Mondays in May
WHERE—Board of Equalization (county); Oregon Tax Court (Small Claims Division) or State Dept. of Revenue; if State Department of Revenue, then Oregon Tax Court

ADMISSIBLE GROUNDS—If higher than legal standard; assessment-sales ratio admissible

PARTIAL/FULL VALUE—The assessment standard is (100%) true cash (market) value; assessment level studies are primarily for use of the Board of Equalization and the Department of Revenue to determine which properties are not being assessed at 100% of true cash value so adjustments may be made to bring them up to the legal standard; agricultural and forest land assessed on use; residences in commercial or industry zone specially assessed at lower rates

TAX RELIEF—"Homestead" tax refund program for homeowners and renters, based on income; "circuit-breaker" innovative property tax deferral (total) for aged 62 and over who live in their residences; property tax payments are merely delayed, however, and must be paid when the owner dies or ownership changes; no income minimums or maximums

ASSESSORS—33 elected, 3 appointed; must meet educational and experience standards

MANUAL—No single state assessment manual; however, Oregon has a full overall innovative instructional guidance program and public set of publications for its assessors and an excellent informational set of publications for its taxpayers, even descriptive cartoon publications

PENNSYLVANIA

WHEN TO APPEAL—Before 30 days from assessment notice

WHERE—Board of Assessment Appeals (county) or Board of Revision (county)

ADMISSIBLE GROUNDS—If higher than legal standards; if higher than nearby similar property; if higher than legal average for district; assessment-sales ratio admissible

PARTIAL/FULL VALUE—Actual value in some localities, 75% in others

TAX RELIEF—"Circuit-breaker" relief to homeowners 65 and over and totally disabled

ASSESSORS—Elected and appointed; no qualifications necessary

RHODE ISLAND

WHEN TO APPEAL—Before 60 days after publication of tax roll

WHERE—Board of Assessment and Review or County Superior Court

ADMISSIBLE GROUNDS—Assessment-sales ratio not admissible

PARTIAL/FULL VALUE—Full value

TAX RELIEF—Homeowners 65 and over; varying formulas

ASSESSORS—Appointed

SOUTH CAROLINA

WHEN TO APPEAL—Before 10 days from day of assessment

WHERE—Board of Equalization, South Carolina Tax Commission; Tax Board of Equalization (state)

ADMISSIBLE GROUNDS—Assessment-sales ratio admissible

PARTIAL/FULL VALUE—Homes—40% of full market value; manufacturing real and personal—10.5%; agricultural—4% of use value; merchants inventory—6%; transportation companies—9.5%

TAX RELIEF—For aged 65 and older, first $10,000 of value is exempt

ASSESSORS—Appointed, no qualifications necessary

MANUAL—No

SOUTH DAKOTA

WHEN TO APPEAL—Between February 1st and May Board Meeting

WHERE—Board of Equalization (local); County Board of Equalization; State Tax Board of Equalization

ADMISSIBLE GROUNDS—If higher than nearby similar property; assessment-sales ratio admissible

PARTIAL/FULL VALUE—Homes assessed on full value basis; recent assessment to sales price ratio is 80%; county committee sets level of taxable value; agricultural land is assessed on market value and "capability"

TAX RELIEF—Program is based on age and income

ASSESSORS—Appointed; no qualifications necessary; must become state certified in 2 years; term is 2 years, probation 1st year

MANUAL—Yes

TENNESSEE

WHEN TO APPEAL—Between June 1st to session's end

WHERE—Board of Equalization (county)

ADMISSIBLE GROUNDS—If higher than legal standard; if higher than nearby similar property; assessment-sales ratio admissible

PARTIAL/FULL VALUE—Full value then class percentages as follows:

	REAL PROPERTY	TANGIBLE PERSONAL PROPERTY
Public Utilities	55%	55%
Commercial/Industrial	40%	30%
Residential	25%	5%
Farm	25%	5%

Recent sales ratios range from 48% to 90% of market value

TAX RELIEF—Tax rebate program for low-income elderly, disabled veterans

ASSESSORS—Elected for 4 years; no qualifications necessary

MANUAL—Yes

TEXAS

WHEN TO APPEAL—Before 2nd Monday in May

WHERE—Board of Equalization (county)

ADMISSIBLE GROUNDS—If higher than legal standard; if higher than nearby similar property; if higher than average for district; assessment-sales ratio not admissible

PARTIAL/FULL VALUE—True full value is maximum

TAX RELIEF—Homeowners 65 and over; flat deduction in assessment not based on income

ASSESSORS—Elected and appointed; no qualifications necessary

UTAH

WHEN TO APPEAL—Between May 31 and June 20th

WHERE—Board of Equalization (county), State Tax Commission

ADMISSIBLE GROUNDS—If higher than legal standard; if higher than nearby similar property; assessment-sales ratio admissible

PARTIAL/FULL VALUE—Home value determined on full value basis, then 20% percentage assigned; recent state *average* assessment level 13.98%

TAX RELIEF—Tax rebates for owners and renters of residences aged 65 and over, based on income

ASSESSORS—Elected for 4 years; no qualifications necessary

MANUAL—No

VERMONT

WHEN TO APPEAL—Varying dates

WHERE—Board of Assessors (local); Board of Civil Authority (local)

ADMISSIBLE GROUNDS—If higher than legal standard; if higher than nearby similar property; if higher than average for district; assessment-sales ratio admissible. Local Board of Assessors rarely grant appeals because they judge their own work; higher appeals are more successful

PARTIAL/FULL VALUE—By state law, all classes determined at full value then 50% percentage applied

TAX RELIEF—"Circuit-breaker" for all homeowners and renters, based on income

ASSESSORS—Elected for 3 years; no qualifications necessary

MANUAL—Yes

VIRGINIA

WHEN TO APPEAL—Between January 1st and June 30th in cities, all year long in counties

WHERE—City or County Board of Equalization

ADMISSIBLE GROUNDS—If higher than legal standard; if higher than nearby similar property; if higher than average for district; assessment-sales ratio admissible

PARTIAL/FULL VALUE—All classes assessed at 100% fair market value by law; agricultural and open space lands assessed on use-value basis

TAX RELIEF—Those aged 65 and older and handicapped, tax relief based on income and net worth

ASSESSORS—Appointed and elected; no qualifications necessary

MANUAL—No

WASHINGTON (State)

WHEN TO APPEAL—Before July 15th

WHERE—Board of Equalization (county); State Board of Tax Appeals

ADMISSIBLE GROUNDS—If higher than legal standard; if higher than nearby similar property; if higher than average for district; assessment-sales ratio admissible

PARTIAL/FULL VALUE—All classes except utilities assessed at full value; latest assessment-sales ratio, state average was 80.2%; state ratio determinations are made by county only

TAX RELIEF—Senior citizens and disabled owners or renters of residences or mobile homes; tax relief based on income

ASSESSORS—Elected for 4 years and must pass state certification exam

MANUAL—No (uses Marshall & Swift Cost Service)

WASHINGTON (District of Columbia)

WHEN TO APPEAL—First Monday in January to April 15th

WHERE—Board of Equalization and Review

ADMISSIBLE GROUNDS—If higher than legal standard; if higher than similar nearby property; assessment-sales ratio admissible

PARTIAL/FULL VALUE—Full value in cash

TAX RELIEF—"Circuit-breaker" for homeowners and renters; variable, based on income

ASSESSORS—Appointed D.C. officials

WEST VIRGINIA

WHEN TO APPEAL—Before February 28th

WHERE—County Commission (in its capacity as Board of Equalization and Review)

ADMISSIBLE GROUNDS—If higher than legal standard; if higher than nearby similar property; if higher than average for district; assessment-sales ratio admissible

PARTIAL/FULL VALUE—All classes determined on full-value basis, then different rates apply to different classes; latest ratio of assessed to sales value was 35%

TAX RELIEF—"Circuit-breaker" for aged 65 and over and less than $5000 gross income; "Homestead" exemption for aged 65 and over, $5,000 reduction in primary residence assessed value

ASSESSORS—Elected 4-year term, no qualifications necessary

MANUAL—Yes (advisory only)

WISCONSIN

WHEN TO APPEAL—Before 1st week from 2nd Monday in July

WHERE—Local Board of Relief; State Department of Revenue

ADMISSIBLE GROUNDS—If higher than legal standard; if higher than nearby similar property; if higher than average for district; assessment-sales ratio admissible

PARTIAL/FULL VALUE—Full value

TAX RELIEF—Homeowner's exemption for aged 65 and over, based on income; homeowner's and renter's "circuit-breaker," based on income

ASSESSORS—Elected and appointed

WYOMING

WHEN TO APPEAL—Between 4th May Monday and 2nd June Monday

WHERE—Board of Equalization (county); State Board of Equalization

ADMISSIBLE GROUNDS—If higher than similar nearby property; assessment-sales ratio admissible

PARTIAL/FULL VALUE—25% basis, except mineral production at 100%; agricultural lands on a productivity basis

TAX RELIEF—None (repealed 1977 in favor of a sales tax rebate varying with income)

ASSESSORS—Elected 4-year terms, no qualifications necessary

MANUAL—Yes (Building Cost Manual)

Appendix II

AN ADDRESS LIST OF STATE OFFICIALS

Chief
Ad Valorem Tax
Division
Alabama Dept. of
Revenue
Montgomery, Alabama
36102

State Assessor
Dept. of Comm & Reg
Affrs
Div. of Local Govt.
Ass't.
P.O. Box 710
Juneau, Alaska 99801

Director
Division of Property
and Special Taxes
Dept. of Revenue
Phoenix, Arizona
85038

Director
Assessment Coord. Div.
Dept. of Comm.—Exec.
Bldg.
2020 W 3rd St.
Little Rock, Arkansas
72205

Chief
Div. of Assessment
Standards
State Board of Equal.
P.O. Box 1799

Sacramento, California
95808

Property Tax
Administrator
Dept. of Local Affrs.—
Prop. Tax
614 Capitol Annex
Denver, Colorado
80203

Municipal Assessment
Agent
State Tax Dept.
92 Farmington Avenue
Hartford, Connecticut
06115

Director
Ad Valorem Tax
Bureau
State Dept. of Revenue
Room 230 Carlton
Bldg.
Tallahassee, Florida
32304

Director of Equalization
Georgia Dept. of
Revenue
Trinity-Washington
Bldg.
Atlanta, Georgia 30334

Asst. Dir.—Tax.
Property Technical
Office

Hawaii Dept. of
Taxation
P.O. Box 259
Honolulu, Hawaii
96809

State Tax Commission
Property Division
P. O. Box 36
Boise, Idaho 83722

Director
Dept. of Local Govern.
Affrs.
State of Illinois
303 E Monroe St.
Springfield, Illinois
62706

Chairman
State Brd. of Tax
Commissioners
State Office Bldg—Rm.
201
Indianapolis, Indiana
46204

Director
Property Tax Division
Iowa Dept. of Revenue
Lucas State Office Bldg.
Des Moines, Iowa
50319

Director
Div. Prop. Val.—Dept.
of Rev.

State Office Bldg.
Topeka, Kansas 66612

Director
Property & Inheritance
Tax Div.
Kentucky Dept. of Rev.
State Capitol
Frankfort, Kentucky
40601

Chairman
Louisiana Tax
Commission
P. O. Box 44244—
Capitol Station
Baton Rouge, Louisiana
70804

State Tax Assessor
Bureau of Taxation
State Office Bldg.
Augusta, Maine 04330

Deputy Director
Dept. of Assessments &
Tax.
301 West Preston St.
Baltimore, Maryland
21201

Associate Commissioner
Div. of Local Finance
Dept. of Corp. & Tax.
100 Cambridge St.
Boston, Massachusetts
02204

Executive Secretary
State Tax Commission
Dept. of Treasury—
Treas. Bldg.
Lansing, Michigan
48922

Director
Prop. Equal Div.—State
Dept. of Tax.
Centennial Office Bldg.
St. Paul, Minnesota
55145

Ad Valorem
Commissioner
State Tax Commission
P.O. Box 960
Jackson, Mississippi

Chairman
State Tax Commission
State Capitol
Jefferson City, Missouri
65101

Director
Property Tax Field
Program
Dept. of Rev.—Mitchell
Bldg.
Helena, Montana
59601

Administrator
Prop. Tax Div.—Dept.
of Revenue

P.O. Box 94818
Lincoln, Nebraska
68509

Director
Div. of Assessment
Standards
Dept. of Tax.
Carson City, Nevada
89701

Secretary
Dept. of Rev. Adm.
State Office Bldg.
Concord, New
Hampshire 03301

Director
Property Tax Dept.
Bataan Memorial Bldg.
Santa Fe, New Mexico
87503

State Supervisor
Local Prop. & Pub.
Uty. Branch
Div. of Tax.—Dept. of
Treas.
West State & Will
Trenton, New Jersey
08625

Director
State Brd. of Equal. &
Assessment
Agency Bldg. #4
Empire St. Plz.
Albany, N.Y. 12223

Secretary
State Board of Assess
Dept. of Rev.
P. O. Box 25000
Raleigh, North
Carolina 27640

Assessment Supervisor
Office State Tax
Commr.
State Capitol
Bismarck, North
Dakota 58501

Chief
Prop. Tax Div.—Ohio
Tax Dept.
P. O. Box 530
Columbus, Ohio 43216

Director
Ad Valorem Division
Oklahoma Tax
Commission
2101 Lincoln
Boulevard
Oklahoma City,
Oklahoma 73194

Administrator
Assessment & Appraisal
Div.
Oregon Dept. of Rev.
504 State Office Bldg.
Salem, Oregon 97310

Chairman
State Tax Equal Board

Box 1294
Harrisburg,
Pennsylvania 17108

Supervisor
Tax Equal. Section
Dept. of Community
Affairs
150 Washington St.
Providence, Rhode
Island 02808

Director
Property Tax Division
State Tax Comm.
Box 125
Columbia, South
Carolina 29214

Prop. Tax Div.
State Dept. of Revenue
State Capitol Bldg.
Pierre, South Dakota
57501

Director
Div. of Prop.
Assessment
Office of State Comptr.
289 Plus Park Blvd.
Nashville, Tennessee
37217

Director
Ad Valorem Tax Div.
Comptr. of Pub. Accts.
State of Texas—Capitol
Bldg.

Austin, Texas 78711

Director
Local Val. Div.—State
Tax Comm.
2870 Connor St.
Salt Lake City, Utah
84109

State Tax Commissioner
Dept. of Taxation
P. O. Box 6-L
Richmond, Virginia
23215

Assistant Director
Prop. Taxes—St. Dept.
of Rev.
General Adm. Bldg.
Olympia, Washington
98504

Director
Local Govern. Rel. Div.
State Tax Dept.
301 Capitol Bldg.
Charleston, West
Virginia 25305

Director
Prop. & Util. Tax
Bureaus
Dept. of Revenue
1000 State Office Bldg.
Madison, Wisconsin
53702

Director
  Ad Valorem Tax Dept.
  Dept. of Revenue and
  Tax
  2200 Carey Avenue
  Cheyenne, Wyoming
  82002

Assessment Standards
  Specialist
  Dept. of Finance &
  Revenue
  Rm. 4126 Municipal
  Center
  300 Indiana Avenue,
  NW

Washington, D.C.
20001

Director
  Div. of Rev.—St. Dept.
  of Finance
  601 Delaware Avenue
  Wilmington, Delaware
  19899

Property Tax Division
  Dept. of Taxes
  State Office Building
  Montpelier, Vermont
  05602

Appendix III

An Assessment Dictionary

The foregoing chapters have given you the theory and tools to do a property tax appeal. This Dictionary gives you the correct words to prepare your appeal, using construction, assessment and appraisal terms properly. It will help you understand the whole process of assessing and taxing. It will also enable you to use the right word in the right place for a correct and persuasive property tax appeal.

A DICTIONARY OF
APPRAISAL, ASSESSMENT AND PROPERTY TAX
TERMS

AGE—*Actual age* is the number of years since building was erected; *effective* age is what a building exhibits based on the state of its modernization.

AD VALOREM TAX—A tax which is based on the value of the property.

AIR RIGHTS—The right to use the space over a land parcel above a certain height.

AMENITIES—In property, those features which benefit and give added value to the ownership.

APPRAISAL—A property valuation.

ASSESSMENT—The value of a property which is multiplied by a tax rate to get the dollar tax amount.

ASSESSMENT DISTRICT—The area which is controlled by the assessor.

ADVERSE INFLUENCES—Factors which affect value such as heavy traffic, odors, smoke, unsightly views, etc.

ASSESSMENT PERIOD—The time frame within which the assessor must assess all properties in his area.

ASSESSMENT-SALES RATIO—A statistical review which compares the recent sales price of properties to their assessments. The resulting average percentage, usually well below 100%, is the assessment-sales ratio. In some states, such as New York, this ratio is available from the state and can be used in an appeal.

ASSESSMENT ROLL—The legal list of all properties together with the assessment value for each one of the listed properties in the assessment area.

ASSESSOR—The official, elected or appointed, who is legally responsible for assessing properties for ad valorem taxes.

CAPITALIZATION—An arithmetical process for deriving total property value by multiplying its net income by a factor; for example, $10,000 net income by 11 = $110,000 value

CIRCUIT-BREAKER LAWS—State laws which limit the amount of taxes which can be charged to certain property owners, usually on dwellings, with the tax relief declining as household income rises.

CLASSES OF TAX—Property tax system where assessment rate is different for different property types.

COST APPROACH—An old-fashioned appraisal method still used by many assessors who estimate the land value, then add the depreciated replacement cost of the building to get "market value."

CUBIC CONTENT—Volume of a building measured from outer surfaces of walls and roof down to lowest floor.

DEED—A written legal paper which describes and transfers the property ownership, usually legally recorded with copy kept on file in local municipal land office records.

DEPRECIATION—Describes value which is lost to the property from various factors such as *physical* (age, wear and tear), *functional* (old fashioned design and equipment), *economic* (adverse factors outside of property lines on block, in area, or in real estate sales activity).

ECONOMIC LIFE—An old-fashioned appraisal guess still used by many appraisers and assessors to predict how long a property's value will endure.

ENCROACHMENT—That portion of a building improvement which lies on another's land.

EQUALIZATION—Function usually performed by state boards to try to equalize different communities' property taxes. This is usually done by comparing actual market sale prices to assessment amounts and then using resulting equalization rates to apportion state aid moneys to each community and for other purposes.

EXEMPTIONS—Certain partial or full tax exemptions for religious institutions, veterans, etc.

FULL VALUE ASSESSMENT REQUIREMENTS—Describes those regulations which require that assessments be at full market value. (See "Partial Value.")

GRANTEE—The one who receives the ownership or deed to a property, the buyer.

GRANTOR—The one who gives the ownership or deed to a property, the seller.

GROSS INCOME—The total income generated by a piece of property.

GROSS INCOME MULTIPLIER—An old-fashioned appraisal method sometimes still used which multiplies the income by a factor to get value of the property; ie. $350 monthly rent × 120 (factor) = $42,000. Not recommended.

IMPROVED PROPERTY—Land "improved" with buildings, driveways, landscaping, etc.

HIGHEST AND BEST USE—Property has to be assessed at its best and most profitable use.

"HOMESTEAD" LAWS—State laws which exempt certain properties certain amounts, as in Alabama, which gives $2000 "homestead" assessment deduction for properties or those portions of properties used for dwelling purposes.

INCOME APPROACH—A standard appraisal approach to value, generally used for commercial, industrial and large multiple dwellings when similar property sales are not available. The net income real or expected is multiplied by a capitalization factor to get total property value. (See "Capitalization.") This approach is not useful for 1-4 family dwellings.

LAND RESTRICTIONS—Legal restrictions on a parcel's use may be by deed or by municipal zoning.

LEASE—A written document given by a *lessor* to a *lessee* for the lessee to use a property for a specific time under particular conditions and cost.

LEASEHOLD—The property which is leased.

LEASEHOLD IMPROVEMENTS—Buildings, alterations, etc. done by a lessee during lease.

LEGAL DESCRIPTION—A property's legal written description which recites its outside boundaries. (See "Deed.")

MARKET VALUE—Market value is that amount which a

property will bring in the open market from a ready, willing and able buyer and a willing seller, neither acting under duress or constraint.

MORTGAGE—The legal document which the property owner gives to the bank or creditor who lends him money for buying the property or for other purpose, using the property as security for the loan.

NON-CONFORMING USE—A legal use of a property because that use existed before zoning regulations forbid that use.

OPERATING EXPENSES—Those expenses, operating costs and reserves which are deducted from gross income to secure net income. (See Income Approach.)

OVER-ASSESSED—A property which is assessed too high.

PERSONALTY—Personal property not attached to and not part of the real estate.

PARCEL OR PROPERTY NUMBER—An identification number, such as Section, Block and Lot number, which is used in many taxing districts to identify parcels.

PROPERTY RECORD CARD—A public record card which assessor keeps in his file to record descriptive and assessment data on each property.

REAL ESTATE—All the land and improvements within the property.

REAL PROPERTY—Defined generally as including all the rights ownership of real estate gives the owner. (For example, see "Air Rights.")

RELIEF—Various state laws which afford certain taxpayers "homestead," "senior citizen" or other tax deductions.

REVALUATION—The reassessment of all properties in a taxing area.

REPLACEMENT and REPRODUCTION COST—Two terms involved in the Cost Approach system. Replacement cost means calculating how much it would cost to reproduce a property with equal modern materials; reproduction, how much with the same materials. (see "Cost Approach.")

SQUARE FEET—When applied to buildings, exterior measurements of each floor of livable area.

TAX DISTRICT—The geographical municipal taxing area which is assessed.

TAX LEVY—The total dollar amount which has to be raised legally from taxes, needed to pay the community's expenses.

TAX MAP—A community map or maps which show all the parcels being taxed.

TAX NOTICE—The legally required notice to the owner of a revaluation of his property.

TAX RATE—This rate is secured by dividing the total assessed value of the district into the tax levy and is usually expressed in dollars per hundred or per-thousand. This rate is then multiplied by the assessed value to get amount of taxes on each property. For example, $1,500,000 tax levy ÷ $75,000,000 = $20 per $1000 tax rate. Thus, a house assessed @ $50,000 multiplied by $20 tax rate would pay $1000 a year taxes.

TAX ROLL—Same as Assessment Roll.

UNDER-ASSESSED—When property assessment is too low compared to similar properties.

VALUATION—Same as Appraisal.

ZONING REGULATIONS—Municipal restrictions on land use.

Index

ABOUT THE AUTHOR

Samuel T. Barash is the author of *Standard Real Estate Appraising Manual*, Prentice-Hall, 1979. As a government and independent real estate appraiser, developer and broker for 30 years, he appraised, sold, subdivided and developed residential, commercial and industrial properties in New York, New Jersey, Pennsylvania and Massachusetts. This included 15 years as cost estimator, inspector, chief of construction and supervisory appraiser for the New York office of the Veterans Administration as well as seven years as VA chief appraiser in New Jersey. He has been qualified as an expert appraisal witness in many state and federal courts including numerous assessment appeals involving investigation, appraisal reports and testimony.